How to Trace Your Family Tree

How to Trace Your Family Tree

David Poteet

Jeremy Books
5624 Lincoln Drive Edina, Minnesota 55436

5624 Lincoln Drive Edina, Minnesota 55436

Second edition 1979

Printed in the United States of America

Library of Congress Catalog Card Number: 79-84344
ISBN 0-89877-002-3
Cartoon designs by Joe Plott

TABLE OF CONTENTS

Introduction

Tracing your family tree is a great deal of fun. Not only do you find out who many of your ancestors were, you can also learn more about the history of our country (and other countries) as you discover where your relatives lived and what they did. American history will come alive to you and your children as you follow your ancestors' lives. You might find a famous ancestor somewhere in the past. You might even uncover character traits in your family that will help you understand yourself. True, this involves work and sometimes frustration, but the rewards are great.

Genealogy has had a lasting significance in nearly all civilizations. One indication of this is the prominent place the Bible gives it; you have only to think of all the begats: Abraham begat Isaac, Isaac begat Jacob, and so on. In the New Testament, the first thing you find in the gospel of Matthew is Jesus' genealogy. All this indicates that much of a person's significance and identity in Jewish society, and in many societies, is closely related to the families from which he or she is descended.

Another benefit of tracing your ancestors is the challenge involved. You become a detective as you search through records, as you try to trace some missing ancestor, as you attempt to piece together facts. I once had the pleasure of uncovering the truth about a man who founded a flintlock rifle manufacturing plant in the early 1800's. The only history book that mentioned him passed him off as a thief. In his diary, in the company's records, and in newspaper accounts, I found that he was an honorable man who had been falsely accused of doctoring his records, and other crimes. I found records of a court trial that proved him innocent. The genuine thrill I felt when I found out the truth was plenty of reward for all the work involved.

When you have stuck to what will sometimes be a frustrating task, when you have followed up a dozen false leads, written countless letters, when you have gone through all this and have succeeded, even in only one line, your sense of accomplishment will amply repay you for it all.

So be prepared for work and for rewards. You'll experience both.

Chapter One
How To Begin

1. MOVE FROM THE PRESENT TO THE PAST.

The most important rule of genealogical research is this: *begin with yourself and work back through time*. If you ignore this rule and begin with, for example, the Revolutionary War, writing down every soldier who has your family's name, you'll probably wind up with a long list of names, but with no way to connect them to one another.

Several reasons make it almost impossible to connect the people on such a list. The first is that when you get two or three hundred years back in your family tree, you have so many cousins, uncles, and other relatives of the same name, finding your exact line from that starting point is almost impossible.

The second reason is that many families have the same last name but are not related. In the Middle Ages a man took his last name from his occupation, or from where he lived, or from some physical characteristic, or from some other source. If he was a blacksmith, he took the name Smith; if he drove carts, he called himself Carter; if he was a woodworker, he might call himself Turner, or Carpenter; if he was tall, he might be called Long, if short, Little (Poteet means "little" in French), and so on. Can you imagine how many turners or smiths or carpenters you could find in the Middle Ages, almost all of them unrelated to one another? So, someone of your family name may or may not be related to you.

A final reason relates to immigration to America. Often, immigrants would take or were given an English-sounding name. For instance, a man whose father's original name was something like Poniatowski came to America and the immigration officials gave him the name Farrell. However, being named Farrell certainly did not make him a relative of the Farrells. Amusingly, his son recently received a letter from one of those questionable companies which send out family coats of arms to everyone of a certain name. The company congratulated the younger Farrell on being descended from the well-known Irish family of Farrell, and offered (for a fee of course) to send him his family tree. He got quite a laugh from that. So, be careful about assuming that all Farrells are Irish, or that everyone with your last name is related to you.

Always begin with yourself. You already know where your mother and father were born, as well as other information about them. You may know much about your grandparents. That's where to start. Armed with that basic information, work backwards in time, and you will be able to trace your family tree much more easily and accurately than by starting with some immigrant who happens to have your last name.

2. KEEPING RECORDS.

The simplest way to keep your records is in a standard three-ring notebook, available from any office supply company. Get a good quality notebook, because it may see some hard use. Use lined 8 ½ x 11 paper (the type used by college students) that has narrower spaces between the lines; you can get more on a page with this type of paper.

In the upper right-hand corner of every page you use, write down two basic items of information: first, the subject (it may be a specific individual or a whole family); second, a coded reference showing how that person is related to you. With this information in the upper right-hand corner of each page, one glance will tell you which relative is recorded on that page.

The following code works well, but feel free to work out your own system. Let F stand for father, M for mother, S for sister, B for brother, H for husband, W for wife, C for cousin, ML for mother-in-law, and so on. Using these simple symbols, you can create a code that will keep the generations straight. Here is the way it works:

F — Father

2F — Grandfather (father's father)

3F — Great-Grandfather (father's father's father)

4F — Great-Great-Grandfather (father's father's father's father)

and on through as many generations as you need. Notice that beginning with 3F (your great-grandfather), the number of greats before grandfather is always two less than the number in front of the F. For instance, 8F would be your grandfather with six greats in front of it, 13F would have eleven greats in front of grandfather, and so on. This system is much simpler than writing out all those greats every time you refer to an ancestor.

Using this same number-letter combination, you can easily create a code for every ancestor or relative you have. First, record their simple relationship to you, then follow that with a code that shows in more detail how they are related to you. For example:

Suppose you want a code for your great-great-great-grandmother. Her simple code would be 5M. But, since you have a number of great-great-great-grandmothers, how will you know from that reference which one she is? Let's say she is your mother's great-grandfather's mother (in your mother's father's direct line). You would code her M3FM because she is your mother's father's father's father's mother. The complete code you would use for her, containing both her simple relationship to you as well as the code for the more detailed relationship, would be 5M (M3FM).

Here is another example. Let's say you want to code your great-grandfather's first cousin. You can approach this in two different ways. You could code him simply 3F1stC. But, since your great-grandfather's first cousin is also your great-great-grandfather's son, it might be clearer to code him 4FS. Personally, I prefer the more direct code, like this last example, rather than using the term cousin or the symbol for it. I believe you'll find the term "cousin" too vague, so I suggest you avoid it entirely in making up codes for ancestors. In this same example of your great-great-grandfather's son (4FS), if you need to specify which son he was, add that to your code. If he was the second son, his code would read 4F2ndS.

Here is a final example. You may want to code a fairly complicated relationship. Let's use as an example your father's mother's father's mother's mother's brother. In such a case as this, use a direct code, assigning a letter to everyone in the list: his code would be FMFMMB. I think that after you practice assigning these codes a few times, you will get the hang of it. The most basic rule to remember is that beginning with 3F (great-grandfather), the number of greats in front of grandfather is always two less than the number in front of the F.

After you have written the person's name and his code in the upper right-hand corner of the page, add on the rest of that page that person's basic information: birth date and location; whom he or she married; children's names and other information about them; where the family lived (don't forget they might have moved around, hence have had several addresses); employment record; and miscellaneous information. Leave the bottom one-fourth of the page for recording sources in which you found the various information recorded on that page.

You can tie the information you have recorded on the main part of the page to the sources written out at the bottom of the page by using footnotes. If you found your great-grandfather's birth date in the Smith family Bible, record the entry as follows: born January 14, 1867 (1). The number one in parentheses will tie the entry to your source reference at the bottom of the page, which you will record in this way: (1) Smith family Bible. By assigning a number to each entry, then a corresponding number to the source entry at the bottom of the page, you will keep clear records of where you found all your data. Be sure to record sources in detail. Don't write merely *Johnson County Deed Book*. Write the entry in full detail as *Johnson County, Maryland Deed Book No. 4, 1873-1876, page 232*. Write in parentheses after the source entry where it is located, in case you have to go back and look at it again.

Make up one of these sheets, called family group sheets, for each ancestor. Then file each family group sheet in your three-ring notebook according to what family line they represent, then from present to past in that line. It would help you to transfer the names and basic vital statistics of each person you find to a genealogical chart; this will help you keep your ancestors straight, as well as show you what you have accomplished and what remains to be done. Completed charts make welcome presents for your relatives as well. Genealogical charts can be ordered from several sources mentioned in the address section of this book.

Maintain a list of the records you have examined. Keep this on a separate sheet, maybe in the back of your notebook; on it write the specific name of the record you looked at, where you found it, the date you used it, its call number (if any), and briefly, what you found. If you found nothing, note that; it will save you from going back over ground you have already covered.

Near the front of your notebook, have a section where you keep scratch notes to yourself: notes such as ideas, potential sources, other lines to trace, and so on. You might want to use small glue-on tabs for certain key pages, so you can more easily find a family name, or a particular ancestor. Also, you can use several three-ring pocket folders to put miscellaneous notes, copies of articles, etc., into.

Be sure to put your name and address prominently in the front of the notebook on a page you do not remove; that way, if you leave your notes in a library or elsewhere, they can be returned to you. Add a note that if the finder mails it to you, he will get a small reward.

Virtually all archives will require you to use a pencil, not a fountain pen or ballpoint pen. This is because some people absent-mindedly make ink marks on valuable old records. A mechanical pencil with eraser and an extra supply of lead works well.

When you actually begin making notes from a source, say a deed or will book, make complete notes. Copy virtually every word, certainly every important one. If you don't, you may regret it later, for you may need the one piece of information you omitted. You may want to use some abbreviations of your own; just be sure you know what they all mean.

16

(Sample Family Chart)

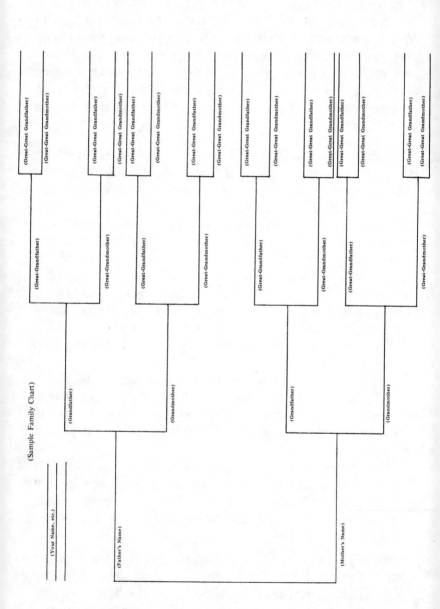

(Your Name, etc.)

(Father's Name)

(Mother's Name)

(Grandfather)

(Grandmother)

(Grandfather)

(Grandmother)

(Great-Grandfather)

(Great-Grandmother)

(Great-Grandfather)

(Great-Grandmother)

(Great-Grandfather)

(Great-Grandmother)

(Great-Grandfather)

(Great-Grandmother)

(Great-Great Grandfather)

(Great-Great Grandmother)

(Great-Great Grandfather)

(Great-Great Grandmother)

(Great-Great Grandfather)

(Great-Great Grandmother)

(Great-Great Grandfather)

(Great-Great Grandmother)

(Great-Great Grandfather)

(Great-Great Grandmother)

(Great-Great Grandfather)

(Great-Great Grandmother)

(Great-Great Grandfather)

(Great-Great Grandmother)

(Great-Great Grandfather)

(Great-Great Grandmother)

(Sample Information Sheet)

Person's Name: Birth Date:
Code: Birthplace:

Death Date:
Burial Location:

Spouse's Name:
Date of Marriage:

Childrens' Names (in order of birth):

   1.
   2.
   3.
   4.
   5.

Where They Lived:

   1.
   2.
   3.
   4.

Education:

Military Service:

Employment:
Sources:

NOTE: If you want to buy either Family Charts, Individual Information Sheets, or Family Group Sheets, you can order them from the New England Historic Genealogical Society, 101 Newbury St., Boston, Mass. 92116. Of course, it would be easy to make your own.

To save time, most libraries or archives offer a reproduction service. At your request (usually you must fill out an order form), they will photostat or Xerox documents for a modest charge. This service is best for longer documents which would take you too long to copy, or when you don't have much time to spend at that location. These copies are usually mailed to you. If they are too large for your notebook, put them in a file folder, and simply label the folder with that person's name and code. You can keep these folders in a filing cabinet or a cardboard box. As a result, all information about that person will be found either in your notebook or in the appropriate file folder.

3. FORM OF THE RECORDS YOU WILL USE.

In libraries, archives, or other places where records are stored, the main records you will be using will be in these forms: books, bound photostatic copies of original records, original records themselves, typed lists, and microfilms. These types of records require careful handling. Some are old and fragile and many are used by large numbers of people and get a lot of wear and tear. Many of these old documents are irreplaceable, and writing on them, or bending or folding them can cause permanent damage. Making sure that you always replace records to their proper place so others can find them when they need them will undoubtedly be greatly appreciated by other "family-tree-tracers."

Some of the records you'll use will be on microfilm. This is especially true of deed books, will books, certain court records, etc. Each reel of microfilm is about three inches in diameter, and contains varying lengths of one-inch wide film. Microfilm can be read only on a microfilm reader. Some libraries expect you to thread your own film in the machine, some want to do it themselves. Don't be afraid of these machines; the people at the desk will be glad to show you how to install the film and use the machine. Ask the staff anything you have questions about. Some archives and libraries have put time limits on the use of microfilm readers. When your time is up, plan to use other records stored there that are not on microfilm.

4. CONTACTING RELATIVES.

One of the best sources of information about ancestors is your relatives, especially your oldest ones. Find out all you can from them. If you can visit them, do so, armed with notebook and pen or, better yet, with a cassette tape recorder from which you can later make notes. It would help if you would set a definite date to visit them; if you thought of questions ahead of time to ask them; if when the discussion wanders off the track you gently led it back.

Locked in their memories is a storehouse of facts, tales, family legends, and clues that may help you immensely. Ask them what they can tell you about their parents, grandparents, or anyone else in the family. Make careful notes of what they say, just as it comes out. You can organize the information later.

If you can't visit them, write them a letter (be sure to keep a carbon copy of each letter you write for your own records). In the letter, ask for specific information. Don't ask them to tell you all they can remember about grandpa; that's too general. Ask them where and when he was born, when he married, whom he married, where he lived, who his children were, what occupation he had, what he was like, what his hobbies were, when and where he died, what was the cause of his death, where he is buried, and so on. You might arrange these questions on several sheets of paper, first stating the question, then beneath it leaving enough space for the answer. Always be sure to include a stamped, self-addressed envelope with your request. If you think any expense will be involved, send an appropriate amount of money.

In addition to asking for information in person or by letter (or if necessary, by phone), ask if they have any family letters, business records, photos (ask them to identify people in the photos by writing their names on the back), books (sometimes people write the date they acquired the book, what grade they were in when they used it, etc.), furniture, clothing, or other property that once belonged to an ancestor, or a family Bible that has birth and death dates recorded in it, or a trunk of letters, etc. If they won't let you borrow it, ask if you can come to where it is. If they don't have anything themselves, ask them if they know anyone in the family who does.

As you receive answers from relatives (or from friends of relatives), add their new information to your notebook. Be sure to write down the source of this information at the bottom of the family group sheet dealing with that person. In evaluating what relatives tell you, try to distinguish between facts and legends. Treat family traditions and legends with healthy skepticism. Use them for clues, but try to prove such stories from other sources before you accept them as true.

If you have written your relatives or their friends, but have had little success, you might try placing a classified advertisement in the newspaper published in the area where you believe your ancestor lived. Ask for information about specific people, if possible. In addition, try looking in phone books from the same areas. Most public libraries (especially state libraries and the Library of Congress) have large collections of phone books. Many times college and university alumnae offices have them too. If all else fails, call information in your target city or area and ask for the phone number of someone of that name. Call them and ask for leads. You might find some real help this way. If you are on vacation, look in the phone directories of whatever town or city you are in, for names of the families you are searching for. If possible, talk to the postmaster or to a general store owner there. They can be gold mines of information.

Cemeteries can be very helpful, if you can find out where your ancestors are buried. Ask those you write if they know of a family cemetery, or a place where someone is likely to be buried. Visit such locations if possible, getting advance permission where necessary. (See the later section on cemeteries for more hints about visiting them).

At the same time you are contacting relatives, you can begin trying to find information from various records on file in national, state, or local depositories.

5. TYPES OF DEPOSITORIES WHERE
RECORDS CAN BE FOUND.

Here are the main places where you are likely to find useful records (addresses for most of these are listed later in this book):

NATIONAL (In scope, with a great variety of records):
>   National Archives, Washington, D.C.
>   Library of Congress, Washington, D.C.
>   National Genealogical Society Library, Washington, D.C.
>   Library of the National Society, Daughters of the American Revolution, Washington, D.C.
>   New York Public Library
>   New York Genealogical and Biographical Society
>   Mormon files, Salt Lake City, Utah
>   The various Regional Federal Records Depositories

STATE:
>   State Archives
>   State Libraries

LOCAL, OTHER:
>   Local Public Libraries
>   College and University Libraries
>   Historical Societies, and Societies such as the United Daughters of the Confederacy, etc.
>   Churches, both local churches, and their national offices
>   Private collections or museums

HOW TO USE THESE: Either go to them in person, or write them. If you visit in person, be sure to ask the personnel there for help. Describe what you're looking for, give them as much specific information as you can, and don't be afraid to ask them for help at every point where you have questions or confusion. Their job is to help you, so don't be timid, even if you feel ignorant.

If you write a library or archives, please remember one important point; such organizations never do genealogical research for you. They will answer a specific question ('Do you have a copy of the will of Henry Braxton, who died in Amherst County, Virginia, in 1887?'), or, at your request, most of them will send you a list of professional genealogists who will research your family tree for you for a fee. Most archives also have free pamphlets describing genealogical records there; ask for one when you write.

Of all the various records depositories, the state archives is one of the most useful. Ordinarily, it will have copies of nearly all county records still existing, as well as official state records of all sorts; in additions, some churches, as well as private individuals, may have donated their records to it. If you must travel some distance to search for appropriate records and you have only limited time, go to the state archives. Be sure to ask the archivists there for help.

Incidentally, if you live at a distance from a state or national library, it is possible to sign out books and sometimes microfilm from them through Inter-Library Loan. Ask your local librarian how to use the Inter-Library Loan service there.

Besides the state library or archives, you should not overlook your local library, no matter how small it may be. Many libraries have special genealogical sections. If your own local library has little of any help, drive to the nearest city of any size and visit its library.

6. SEEKING CLUES FROM HISTORY.

A good American history text will help you a great deal, especially as you get to the 19th or the 18th centuries. Your local public library should have one you can borrow. If you want to buy one, look in a nearby private bookstore or university bookstore; if that is not convenient, you can order this book through any bookstore: *The Oxford History of the American People*, by Samuel Eliot Morison, published by Oxford University Press, 1600 Pollitt Drive, Fair Lawn, New Jersey 07410. Another book you would do well to at least read, if not buy, is *Three Generations In 20th Century America*, by John Clark and others. This is published by Dorsey Press, 1818 Ridge Street, Homewood, Illinois 60430. It traces seventeen families of many backgrounds through three generations.

As you read your American history book, read with the question in mind, 'what might my ancestors have been doing, or where would they have gone during that period?' Ask yourself, did one of them fight in the Korean War, World War II, World War I, Spanish-American War, Civil War, War of 1812, Revolutionary War, or the Colonial Wars?

Wherever he lived, did he engage in some kind of activity that would have been recorded officially: did he own land, pay personal property taxes, own a business, appear in court for a lawsuit, guardianship, or criminal charge; would he have been a church member or have been baptized; would he have belonged to a fraternal order such as the Masons; could he have immigrated from another country and so have immigrant records; could he have gotten his name in the newspapers; could any school records be found for him; did he marry, and could you find the marriage announcement or official records; could he be found in some kind of business records; would his name appear in a history of that county; did he leave a will; and so on. As you can see, the possibilities are endless. Use your imagination to come up with possibilities of your own.

7. PUBLISHED GENEALOGIES.

Some families have already been traced and the results compiled in various ways. Some have been published in book form, some as booklets or large pamphlets, others have been mimeographed, put in some sort of binding, and privately distributed within that family. Sometimes family trees of this last type find their way into various depositories such as public libraries, historical societies, state libraries, or state archives; there, they are often listed under the entry 'Genealogical Notes'.

If you find that all or part of your family has been traced already, be glad, but also be careful. You can trust the work reasonably well if a professional genealogist did it. Most often, though, some member of that family compiled the information, and you have no way of knowing whether he was thorough and careful or not. If you have such a family-prepared work, use it as a starting place, but check at each point to be sure the record is accurate (one indication of accuracy is the frequent presence of specific references to sources of the information).

All I have just said stems from another basic rule about genealogy that you should know and put into practice: *trust only the original records themselves and what they can teach you; look with suspicion on all secondary sources (what someone else has written based on the original sources).* A lot of people do with family trees what they do with the Bible: they take a few facts and draw all sorts of conclusions, some of which are simply wrong. So, in as many cases as possible, base your own work on the original records.

Where can you find out whether or not your family tree has already been compiled? Write or visit the state library or state archives of the state you are researching, and ask them whether or not your family tree has been published in some form, or if they have books listing published family histories from that state. Also, look in Marion J. Kaminkow's *Genealogies In The Library of Congress, A Bibliography* (Baltimore, Md.: Magna Carta Book Co., 1972) (2 Volumes). Kaminkow lists genealogies alphabetically by family name, so is easy to use. However, the books he mentions can be used only in the Library of Congress itself; they cannot be obtained by Inter-Library Loan. If you find your family name in Kaminkow but are unable to travel to the Library of Congress, you should ask your state library or archives if it has a copy of the book you want.

Another source you should check is the index to the large collection of genealogical records compiled by the Mormons. Of course, they use genealogy for religious purposes, while I believe it can be helpful only for historical and family interest. Nevertheless, they have gathered records on almost 50 million individuals, and more than five million families; in some cases these are published genealogies. Moreover, much of this information is on microfilm, available for purchase or use either in Salt Lake City or in numerous branch genealogical libraries elsewhere in the United States. Write The Genealogical Society, 50 East North Temple Street, Salt Lake City, Utah 84150. Request general information about their holdings, and ask them to send you as many forms GA418, 'Request for Copy of Index

Card or Archive Record' as you need. When they send you these, fill them out and send them back; they will tell you what they have, and how much their various services cost.

Again, lest you become overly excited at finding an already-published history of your family, these secondary works are often of questionable accuracy. Use them as a starting place, but check behind them at every point you can.

8. BASIC USEFUL BOOKS.

You should have access to the following books. If they are not in your local public library, you may want to buy them yourself (by ordering them through your local bookstore or from the publisher). Still better would be to ask your public library to buy them, since they would be helpful to everyone interested in tracing his or her family tree.

a. Harold Lancour, *A Bibliography Of Ship Passenger Lists 1538-1825 Being A Guide To Published Lists Of Early Immigrants To North America* (3rd Edition, Revised and Enlarged by Richard J. Wolfe, with a list of Passenger Arrival Records In The National Archives by Frank A. Bridgers) (N.Y.: The New York Public Library, 1963).

b. Marion Kaminkow, *Genealogies In The Library of Congress, A Bibliography* (Baltimore, Md.: Magna Carta Publishing Co., 1972) (2 Volumes). Very helpful and thorough. Of course, the Library of Congress has many other kinds of records valuable for genealogical research.

c. P. William Filby, *American and British Genealogy and Heraldry (A Selected List of Books)* (Chicago: American Library Association, 1975) (2nd Edition). Excellent; lists and brief comments on books concerning many different kinds of records which might help you. Besides America and British Dominions, it lists sources dealing with Latin America.

d. The following publications of the National Archives:

(1) Meredith B. Colket, Jr., and Frank E. Bridgers, *Guide To Genealogical Records In The National Archives* (Catalog No. GS4.6/2: G28. Stock No. 2202-0016). I recommend that you

buy this inexpensive booklet yourself. It is a very helpful reference tool, and has much detail about various records, especially military records. Send $1.65 (the price at this writing) to the Superintendent of Documents, Government Printing Office, Washington, D.C. 20402.

(2) *Genealogical Records In The National Archives* (free pamphlet—General information leaflet No. 5, revised 1976).

(3) *Genealogical Sources Outside The National Archives* (free pamphlet—General information leaflet No. 6, reprinted 1975).

(4) If you want to order copies of federal records on microfilm, ask the National Archives for their catalog, *National Archives Microfilm Publications*. Most of the microfilms listed in this are not useful for genealogists; a few, however, are, such as ship passenger lists, certain military records, etc.

(5) *Federal Population Censuses 1790-1890; A Catalog Of Microfilm Copies of the Schedules*. This has a breakdown by city and county under each census year. Tells what is available, and how to order desired microfilm.

e. U.S. Bureau of the Census, *Factfinder for the Nation* (CFF 76 No. 2, Issued Sept. 1976). This is an excellent four-page brochure describing census records and their general availability. Free, from the Bureau of the Census, Washington, D.C. 20233.

f. *Harvard Guide To American History* (Revised Edition) (Cambridge, Mass.: The Belknap Press of Harvard University Press, 1974) (2 Volumes). This is an excellent bibliographical guide, with many references to books on state and local history, maps, newspapers, church history, fraternal organizations, and other sources that will be of help to you.

g. Many good, detailed 'how to do genealogical research' books exist. One of the best I've seen is Milton Rubincam, *Genealogical Research: Methods and Sources* (Washington, D.C.: The American Society of Genealogists, 1960). Rubincam is excellent for both American and foreign sources, and he has an especially good rundown on what is available in each state in the U.S.A.

h. For a detailed look at American and Canadian sources and how to use them, see Val D. Greenwood, *The Researcher's Guide To American Genealogy* (Baltimore, Md.: Genealogical Publishing Co., Inc., 1974).

i. You can order the following free pamphlets from the Library of Congress, General Reference and Bibliography Division, Washington, D.C. 20540:

(1) *Reference Services and Facilities of the Local History and Genealogy Room.*

(2) *Guide to Genealogical Research: A Selected List.*

(3) *Surnames: A Selected List of Books.*

" MEMBERS OF MY FAMILY HAVE ALWAYS BEEN ACTIVE IN PUBLIC LIFE ! "

Chapter Two
Primary Sources

Many types of records can be helpful. Some of them you may have heard of, some you may not have. You should consider examining each one of the different types, even ones you think would not be useful; clues come in odd places.

The advantage of the sources in this chapter is that they are all primary sources. This means they are either the original records themselves, or copies of the originals. When you use them, you can be reasonably certain that at least since they were written, no one has altered them or read his own interpretation or prejudices into them. Using primary records permits you to draw your own conclusions more accurately.

Here, in alphabetical order, is an examination of the various kinds of primary sources available to you.

1. BIRTH RECORDS.

Birth records might be found in a variety of depositories. For birth records from the 20th Century, write the U.S. Public Health Service, Washington, D.C., and ask for the pamphlet *Where to Write for Birth and Death Records* (DHEW Pub. No. (HRA) 76-1145, rev. 1976). Ordinarily, a letter to your state's Bureau of Vital Statistics in the state capital will get you what you need. Usually, there is a small charge for copies of birth records.

Different states began requiring statewide recording of vital statistics in different years. In Virginia, the beginning date is

1853. Even then, from 1896 to 1912 there is a gap in the records, due to the state not requiring births to be recorded in those years.

If you find the actual birth certificate, it should give you the parents' names and some information about them, and it might give the grandparents' names, along with other facts about them. If you are seeking a birth record dated before your state began keeping official birth records, you can try a variety of possible sources, such as these: (1) family Bibles; (2) church records; (3) tombstones or cemetery records; (4) family papers, or copies of birth records among family papers; (5) school records; (6) immigration and naturalization records; (7) insurance records; (8) membership records in organizations such as Masons, Elks, etc.; (9) military records; (10) marriage records; (11) published genealogies; (12) *Who's Who* type books; (13) pension applications and records; (14) guardian's records; (15) newspaper obituaries; and other sources.

2. RECORDS PERTAINING TO BLACK AMERICANS.

If you are of black ancestry, you should do your research in the standard records recommended in this chapter, such as wills, deeds, tax records, censuses, and the rest. Until you get back to 1865, these sources should provide most of the information you need. Of course, don't forget that some blacks served in the Union army during the Civil War; look for their military records.

A pamphlet that will help is the National Archives' microfilm catalog titled *Black Studies* (1973). Write the National Archives for this. An additional source you may find helpful when you reach the late 1860's and 1870's is the records of the Freedmen's Bureau. These are available on microfilm at the National Archives, or these films may be purchased. They are listed in the catalog titled *National Archives Microfilm Publications*, under the Department of War, Records of the Bureau of Refugees, Freedmen, and Abandoned Lands (RG 105).

Your search for your ancestors further back than 1865 (that is, before the complete emancipation of the slaves), will run into serious difficulties. The basic problem is twofold: first, records of slave ownership are sketchy, and many of them have been destroyed by time, and so on; second, slaves in most cases were called by their first name only, or by their relationship to their mother or their wife, such as 'Mary's Joe.' Sometimes, of course, they would be known by the name of their master, such as Joe Simmons.

You might find records of slave auctions, bills of sale, plantation records, etc. Look for these in state archives, libraries of black colleges or universities, the Library of Congress, collections of private papers, and business records, as well as the various other sources discussed in this chapter. Finally, talk to older relatives, ask them if they remember anything about the family they heard from their parents or grandparents.

3. CARD FILES.

In most archives and major public libraries, the staffs over the years have assembled card files pertaining to many records on deposit there. Entries in them are nearly always alphabetical. Here is a sample of the subjects of the card files in the Virginia State Archives:

a. Confederate Soldiers (showing unit, and where reference to him is found in the printed records).

b. Genealogical Notes Index.

c. Index of Bible Records on deposit there.

d. Index to some family papers.

e. Bounty Warrants Index.

f. Index to Public Service Claims.

g. Marriage Index.

h. Index to Northern Neck Grants and Surveys.

i 18th Century Virginia Grants and Patents.

j. Land Office Military Certificates.

k. Alphabetical List of Soldiers from Dunmore's War.

l. S. Bassett French Biographical Sketches.

When you get to the library or archives, browse around in

those card files available to the public; also ask the personnel on duty about them. You might find something in them that would really help you.

4. CEMETERIES.

Cemeteries can help in two ways: by cemetery records and by tombstones. Sometimes, if a tombstone has been vandalized, or is too weathered to read, or has simply disappeared, cemetery records (or perhaps funeral directors' records) might help greatly.

Tombstones can provide basic information, if you can read them. If you visit a cemetery, be sure to dress in old clothes, and take along some hedge clippers to cut back brush that may have overgrown the tombstone (one of my ancestor's tombstones was almost completely hidden inside a large shrub). Also take along a stiff brush to brush mud or moss off the inscription; take some chalk to rub in the inscription in case it is hard to read. Have a flashlight or camping lantern along as well; at dusk or at night you can shine this directly on the inscription, or, if it is too worn, you could try shining the light from a side angle; this sometimes highlights worn lettering. Bring a camera along, too. If you go near dusk, have a flash attachment. Even if you do take a picture, be sure to write down carefully everything on the tombstone you can read, in case the photograph turns out badly. Be accurate, for at times a tombstone may be the only record you have of a person.

Several kinds of cemeteries exist: churches often own them; sometimes their cemeteries are located in the churchyard itself, sometimes not far away. My great-grandparents are buried in a church-owned cemetery about 100 yards from the church building itself. Then, some cemeteries are privately owned. Some of these are operated as businesses, some are merely family cemeteries. Others are owned by some government agency—either a town or city, or the federal government.

It is usually acceptable to enter a cemetery owned by a town or city without asking permission first (but look for signs to the contrary). For all other cemeteries, it would be best to ask permission before entering them.

Remember, even tombstone inscriptions can be inaccurate. The stonecutter may have made a mistake (this happens more often than you think), or someone may have simply lied about his age. Use tombstones as sources, but try to verify dates on them from other sources.

5. CENSUS RECORDS.

Some state census records exist; you should write the state archives of the state you're interested in for further information about them. Mostly, though, you will be using federal censuses. Federal census records available to the general public begin with the first census of 1790, and continue every ten years through 1890. For the 1790, 1800, and 1810 censuses, the records for some states and counties are missing. The most serious gap in census records is the 1890 census; it was almost completely destroyed in a fire in Washington, D.C. in 1921. Only a few special census records from 1890 still exist.*

Census records from 1900 through 1970 are not available to the public, except under specific conditions. The 1900 census is beginning to be open to the public, but you would need to ask about it at the library or archives you are using. The purpose of

---

*These are from Perry County, Ala., the District of Columbia, Columbus, Ga., Mound Township, Ill., Rockford, Minn., Jersey City, N.J., Eastchester and Brookhaven Township, N.Y., Cleveland and Gaston Counties, N.C., Cincinnati and Wayne Township, Ohio, Jefferson Township, S. Dak., and Ellis, Hood, Kaufman, Rusk, and Trinity Counties, Texas.

keeping these more recent census records closed to the public is to protect the privacy of the individuals mentioned in them, many of whom are still living. The Bureau of the Census will furnish information from the records of these years only to the person who is mentioned in the census, or to his legal representative (the latter must send the court order that appointed him). If the person has died, any of the following people can request census records pertaining to him, if they send a certified copy of the death certificate: (1) a member of the immediate family, that is, father, mother, child, brother, or sister; (2) the surviving husband or wife; (3) a legal beneficiary who submits adequate proof to that effect.

In most cases, you must also send the exact address at which the person in the census was living; it would help to send as many other facts as you know about the person. Write the Personal Census Service Branch, Bureau of the Census, Pittsburg, Kansas 66762. Ask for an Age Search application form (No. BC-600). There is a modest fee for this search.

Returning to those census records dating from 1790 through 1890, you will find they are not as easy to use as you might think. Unless you know where your ancestor lived—that is, specifically what county, township, or city (and here it would really help to know the ward)—you will have to search many hours to find him or her. One alternative is to write to a company that has put at least some of these censuses for some states on computer, and will search their files for a fee. These companies usually advertize in genealogy magazines.

Some of these early censuses are indexed (particularly 1790), but most of them are not. The 1790 Census, which is indexed, has been published as *Heads of Families at the First Census of the United States Taken in the Year 1790* (12 volumes, Washington, D.C., 1907-08, reprinted 1965-72 by the Reprint Company, Spartanburg, S.C., and by the Genealogical Publishing Co., Baltimore, Md).

The 1810 Census is indexed for Virginia only. A card index for the 1880, 1900, and 1920 Censuses was made during the 1930's, but only the 1880 index is open to the public at this writing. Names on these indexes were arranged according to the

'Soundex' system, which groups all names together that sound alike, regardless of how they are spelled. Although the National Archives no longer handles mail inquiries about census records, the index to the 1880 Census is available on microfilm. This index, however, is not complete; it includes only families with children under ten years of age. In addition, an index exists for the very few surviving census records from 1890 (the whole index includes only 6,160 names).

What information can you find in the census records from the various years? Here is a summary, taken from the Census Bureau's *Factfinder for the Nation* information sheet:

1790 Census—Name of family head, free white males of 16 years and up, free white males under 16, free white females, slaves, other persons.

1800 Census—Name of family head, if white—age and sex, race, slaves.

1810 Census—Name of family head, if white—age and sex, race, slaves.

1820 Census—Name of family head, age, sex, race, foreigners not naturalized, slaves, industry (agriculture, commerce, and manufactures).

1830 Census—Name of family head, age, sex, race, slaves, deaf and dumb, blind, foreigners not naturalized.

1840 Census—Name of family head, age, sex, race, slaves, number of deaf and dumb, number of blind, number of insane and idiotic and whether in public or private charge, number of persons in each family employed in each of six classes of industry and one of occupation, literacy, pensioners for Revolutionary or military service.

1850 Census—Name, age, sex, race, whether deaf and dumb, blind, insane, or idiotic, value of real estate, occupation, birthplace, whether married within the year, school attendance, literacy, whether a pauper or convict. Supplemental schedules for slaves, public paupers, criminals, persons who died during the year.

1860 Census—Name, age, sex, race, value of real estate, value of personal estate, occupation, birthplace, whether married within the year, school attendance, literacy, whether deaf and dumb, blind, insane, idiotic, pauper, or convict, number of slave houses. Supplemental schedules for slaves, public paupers, criminals, persons who died during the year.

1870 Census—Name, age, race, occupation, value of real estate, birthplace, whether parents were foreign born, month of birth if born within the year, month of marriage if married within the year, school attendance, literacy, whether deaf and dumb, blind, insane, or idiotic, male citizens 21 and over, and number of such persons denied the right to vote for other than rebellion. Supplemental schedules for persons who died during the year, paupers, prisoners.

1880 Census—Address, name, relationship to family head, sex, race, age, marital status, month of birth if born within the census year, occupation, months unemployed during the year, sickness or temporary disability, whether blind, deaf and dumb, idiotic, insane, maimed, crippled, bedridden, or otherwise disabled, school attendance, literacy, birthplace of person and parents. Supplemental schedules for the Indian population, for persons who died during the year, insane, idiots, deaf-mutes, blind, homeless children, prisoners, paupers, indigent persons.

1890 Census—Destroyed, except for those few schedules previously mentioned.

1900 Census—Address, name, relationship to family head, sex, race, age, marital status, number of years married, for women—number of children born and number now living ; birthplace of person and parents, if foreign born—year of immigration and whether naturalized; occupation, months not employed, school attendance, literacy, ability to speak English, whether on a farm, home owned or rented and if owned, whether mortgaged. Supplemental schedules for the blind and for the deaf.

1910 Census—Address, name, relationship to family head, sex, race, age, marital status, number of years of present marriage, for women—number of children born and number now living; birthplace and mother tongue of person and parents, if foreign born—year of immigration, whether naturalized, and whether able to speak English (if not, language spoken), occupation, industry, and class of worker, if an employee, whether out of work during year, literacy, school attendance, home owned or rented, if owned—whether mortgaged, whether farm or house, whether a survivor of Union or Confederate Army or Navy, whether blind or deaf and dumb.

1920 Census—Address, name, relationship to family head, sex, race, age, marital status, if foreign born—year of immigration to the U.S., whether naturalized, and year of naturalization; school attendance, literacy, birthplace of person and parents, mother tongue if foreign born, ability to speak English, occupation, industry, and class of worker, home owned or rented, if owned—whether mortgaged, for nonfarm mortgaged—market value, original amount of mortgage, balance due, interest rate.

1930 Census—Address, name, relationship to family head, home owned or rented, value or monthly rental, radio set, whether on a farm, sex, race, age, marital status, age at first marriage, school attendance, literacy, birthplace of person and parents, if foreign born, language spoken in home before coming to U.S., year of immigration, whether naturalized, and ability to speak English, occupation, industry, and class of worker, whether at work previous day (or last regular working day), veteran status, for Indians, whether of full or mixed blood, and tribal affiliation.

1940 Census—Address, home owned or rented, value or monthly rental, whether on a farm, name, relationship to household head, sex, race, age, marital status, school attendance, educational attainment, birthplace, citizenship if foreign born, location of residence 5 years ago and whether on a farm, employment status, if at work, whether in private or nonemergency government work, hours worked in week, if seeking work or on public emergency work, duration of unemployment, occupation, industry, and class of worker, weeks worked last year, income last year.

1950 Census—Address, whether house is on farm, name, relationship to household head, race, sex, age, marital status, birthplace, if foreign born, whether naturalized, employment status, hours worked in week, occupation, industry, and class of worker.

1960 and 1970 Censuses—Address, name, relationship to household head, sex, race, age, marital status.

A number of state and territorial censuses were taken in the years between the regular censuses, particularly in the 19th Century. These are described by Henry J. Dubester in *State Censuses: An Annotated Bibliography of Censuses Taken After the Year 1790, by States and Territories of the United States* (Washington, D.C.: 1948). An appendix in that book provides information on the location of existing records.

Also, the National Archives has some census schedules from odd years: 1857 schedules for Minnesota, 1864, 1866, 1867, and 1869 schedules for Arizona, and 1885 schedules for Colorado, Florida, Nebraska, and New Mexico.

Included under the general heading census schedules are the *Mortality Census Schedules.* These were taken in 1850, 1860, 1870, 1880, and 1885. They list persons who died during the 12 months preceding the taking of the census. Only the 1885 mortality schedules are in the National Archives; the others were given to various non-Federal depositories around the country in 1918 and 1919. To find their location, consult an article entitled "The Mortality Schedules," in *National Genealogical Society Quarterly*, 31: pp. 45-49 (June 1943).

Further details of census and mortality schedules are found in Colket and Bridgers, *Guide To Genealogical Records In The National Archives* (Washington, D.C.: The National Archives, 1964), recommended earlier. The complete catalog of census records available for purchase on microfilm is called *Federal Population Censuses 1790-1890* (Washington, D.C.: National Archives and Records Service, 1976), and is available free from the National Archives. It is broken down by county and independent city, and has microfilm order forms in the back of it. Other references to available census records and indexes on microfilm are in the catalog called *National Archives Microfilm Publications* (Washington, D.C.: National Archives, 1974), and these references are found under the Department of Commerce's Records of the Bureau of the Census, RG 29. Don't forget that copies of most of these microfilms are available in the regional federal records centers, and are also available through Inter-Library Loan.

Two sets of the 1830-1880 Censuses were prepared. One set eventually went to the National Archives. The duplicate sets for 1830 and 1840 were deposited with the Federal district or superior courts. Check with them to see their copies. The duplicate copies for 1850, 1860, 1870, and 1880 went to the county courts; many of the county courts have turned their copies over to the state library or state archives. Check with the archives or library in your state to be sure. See also Kay Kirkham's *The Counties of the United States, Their Derivation and Census Schedules* (Salt Lake City, Utah: Kay Publishing Co., 1961), which shows whether or not records exist.

The National Archives also has a few Indian Censuses: Creeks, 1832; Cherokees, 1835, 1895, and a collection of reels called "Indian Census Rolls, 1884-1940." These are found referred to in the catalog called *National Archives Microfilm Publications*, mentioned above. Look in the section of this catalog titled Department of the Interior, Records of the Bureau of Indian Affairs.

Census records were not always accurate, especially in the early years. Since they took months to complete, people could have moved and been counted twice; the census taker might have found no one at home and simply asked the neighbors for information; the family member giving the information might have been unsure of some ages, or the census taker might have simply put something down to save a trip back.

Caution: it is very difficult and time-consuming to use the census records to find anyone initially. Use the census only after you have generally located a person from other sources. Undertake a blind search of the census records only as an absolutely last resort; otherwise you will waste a great deal of time.

6. CHURCH RECORDS.

Church records, especially concerning ancestors who lived in colonial days, can be extremely valuable. This is because colonies, and later, states, had not yet passed laws requiring the area's government to keep records of vital statistics. This job they often passed to the local churches.

Church records may contain much information about an individual such as: baptismal record (date, names of parents, etc.); marriage date and details; burial date, sometimes with a brief comment about the deceased; confirmation date (the date he or she initially joined the church); information about transferring membership to or from another church; record of church activities (in this category, Quakers and Lutherans are the most complete); membership lists, lists of members thrown out of the church or fined; sometimes, freeing of slaves is recorded (especially in Quaker records); bastard children also appear; sometimes (at least in some Lutheran records), where a person came from in the old country is entered, and you may find other information.

Recognize that your ancestors might be of your own church affiliation, but they easily might have belonged to another denomination. Keep an open mind about this, and search various possibilities where records exist for the time and location you're examining.

Where can such church records be found? In a few cases, they are still kept in the church building itself. More and more, though, individual churches have turned their records over to some depository such as a local historical society, the state library, archives, headquarters or historical section, or a seminary or college of that denomination. In the Virginia State Archives, for example, are records (not all of them complete) dating from colonial days to about 1865, from various churches of these denominations: Baptist, Roman Catholic (usually kept in Latin), Disciples of Christ, Episcopal, Friends (Quaker), Lutheran, German Reformed, Methodist, Presbyterian, and Jewish. Unfortunately, these records are generally not indexed. Along with such records, some families have sent their family

Bibles, or copies of the records pages from them, to the State Archives.

Addresses for the headquarters of existing denominations can be found in Frank S. Mead's *Handbook of Denominations* (N.Y.: Abingdon Press, 1975). Another useful book for general locations is Kay Kirkham's *A Survey of American Church Records, For The Period Before The Civil War, East Of The Mississippi River* (Salt Lake City, Utah: Deseret Book Co., 1959/60). See also Edmund L. Binsfield's article, 'Church Archives in the United States and Canada,' in *American Archivist*, July 1958, Vol. 21, No. 3, pp. 311-332. Val Greenwood also has a very helpful list of locations of church records on pages 390-399 of his *The Researcher's Guide To American Genealogy*.

Church records are called by various names; sometimes they are referred to as Registers, at other times Membership Lists, Vestry Minutes (Episcopal), Session Minutes (Presbyterian), and other names.

If you have searched for church records everywhere you can think of and still have failed to turn up anything, visit the area where your ancestors lived; talk to people there about your problem. Look in church cemeteries there for possible clues, or run an advertisement in the newspaper in that area asking for information about your ancestors and their church ties.

7. CITY COUNCIL RECORDS.

Each city or town accumulates scores of records. If you have exhausted other sources, try writing the city or town and ask them what records are available, where they are kept, when and if they can be examined, and whether or not they are indexed. For New England, especially, look for Town Meeting Records. For other areas, look for Minute Books, etc.

8. CITY DIRECTORIES.

City directories exist for most cities since about 1900. Before then, some cities have them, some do not. These directories (not phone books) list alphabetically all people who live in that city and sometimes its suburbs. Beside each name, they give the street address, name of wife (or husband) and children, place of employment, and other pertinent facts. Directories for a particular city should be in that city's public library, though you may discover gaps in their holdings. If you do, check with the Chamber of Commerce there. Try the State Library, too; sometimes it has them for several cities. In addition, the Library of Congress has a large collection of city directories.

9. COLONIAL RECORDS.

Colonial records are usually incomplete, if they exist at all. Time, fires, and wars have taken their toll of these old records. Those that have survived are in such fragile condition that archives are reluctant to let the public use them. Furthermore, only a few such records are indexed.

Some states, notably Virginia, have taken steps to reconstruct their destroyed colonial archives. Virginia has had a large number of documents copied that are in English libraries, archives, and museums. These duplicated records fall under the general category "Colonial Records Project." Even with these, though, don't expect to find much, unless your ancestor was in the colonial government, or was well-known in some other way. Still, if you have exhausted all other sources, you might want to spend some time exploring in these on the slim chance you would find something.

10. MISCELLANEOUS COUNTY RECORDS.

County governments accumulate many different kinds of records. Besides the major kinds we have looked at elsewhere, they take in miscellaneous supporting documents, notes about this and that, licenses, militia lists, lists of indentured apprentices, and so on. These miscellaneous records sometimes are given to the state archives, sometimes they remain in the county courthouse or elsewhere. Ask the county clerk about them, if you have exhausted all the main sources. Such miscellaneous records might be in dusty boxes, or piled in an attic, or in file cabinets. They are rarely indexed. Use them only as a last resort.

11. COURT RECORDS.

Court records are a valuable, and often-overlooked source of help. I am speaking of courts at every level—town, city, county, state, U.S. District, and national. Such courts have different names: circuit courts, superior courts, chancery courts, district courts, state supreme courts, courts of common pleas, county courts, etc.

In their records appear law suits, court judgments and executions, guardians' accounts, affidavits, summonses, court orders, court fees assessed, divorces, bankruptcies, and records of other legal matters. In addition, Revolutionary War officers received their commissions by the courts in many cases. Records of such appointments would fall under court orders.

Cases in court records almost always are indexed according to both plaintiffs (the ones making the charge or bringing the suit or case), and according to defendants, so be sure to check both alphabetical indexes. Such court records are sometimes bound in photostat form, sometimes they are available on microfilm.

Always be sure to check court records. They can be extremely valuable sources for your search.

12. DEATH RECORDS.

Much of the information in the section on birth records applies to death records as well. In addition to the sources mentioned there, try wills, death certificates (which sometimes give occupation, burial location, etc.), mortality schedules compiled by the Census Bureau (see my section on Census Records), and other sources. The mortality schedules (listing those who died in the 12 months preceding 1850, 1860, 1870, 1880, and 1885) are mostly found in the state where the person died. A few are in the D.A.R. Library in Washington, D.C. (the ones here are Arizona, Colorado, D.C., Georgia, Kentucky, Louisiana, and Tennessee). These mortality schedules are far from complete, so you will probably have to look elsewhere as well.

13. FAMILY RECORDS.

The family Bible is the family record source that comes to most peoples' minds first. Ask your relatives if they have one or more Bibles with birth dates or other information in them. If you find one, be glad, but also be careful. Many times, dates were entered in the family Bible months or even years after the event occurred. One clue that this has been done is if the Bible was published after the birth and other dates recorded in it. Another clue is that several entries were made in the same handwriting using the same ink. This means that someone sat down and decided to enter several dates he had been meaning to write down for a long time. Treat such dates as tentative, and try to prove their accuracy by other records if possible.

Some families have turned their Bibles, or at least copies of the pages bearing birth, death, and other dates, over to local libraries or historical societies, or to that state's state library or archives. If your family doesn't have a Bible, write the various libraries and archives; they may not have it, but you might find something that will help.

Other family records, such as letters, papers, diaries, photographs, unrecorded deeds and wills, diplomas, and so on, can be very valuable helps. These can tell you much about the people themselves, their habits, likes, dislikes, and personalities, and you might find information about where they lived, what they did, and much else besides. Photographs also can be valuable, if they are identified. If no one knows who the old bearded gentleman in the picture is, it doesn't do you much good. Seek help in identifying photos from relatives, people who live in the area where your ancestor did, the postmaster or postmistress (a valuable source of information), the owner of the general store, etc.

14. IMMIGRATION AND NATURALIZATION RECORDS.

Once you trace back to an ancestor who came to America from another country, you can run into serious difficulties. If your ancestor came in the last 75 to 100 years, you should be able to locate his immigration-naturalization records, in most cases. If he or she came prior to the Civil War, though, your problems increase.

The first place to begin, especially if the person came after the Civil War, is with the U.S. Immigration and Naturalization Service, Department of Justice, 425 Eye Street, N.W., Washington, D.C. 20536. Give them whatever facts you have about the person, such as approximately when he or she came, from what country, the name of the ship, or any other data you believe might be helpful.

Next, before 1906, naturalization proceedings could be held in a Federal, State, or local court. Federal court naturalization records (outside the District of Columbia) usually are found in the district court records of the district where the naturalization took place. On the state or local level, check with the clerk of the court there for these records. The WPA Records Inventory (ask about this at the State Library or State Archives) should tell you where such naturalization records were in the late 1930's. For further help on the state or local level, ask at your State Archives.

The censuses can also help. Beginning with the 1850 Census, they generally show birthplace (sometimes birthplace of parents if they were foreign-born), and beginning with the 1900 Census, the year of immigration and other pertinent information (See the section on Census Records for more details).

One of the most helpful books you can find on the subject of early immigration records is Harold Lancour's *A Bibliography of Ship Passenger Lists 1538-1825 Being A Guide To Published Lists Of Early Immigrants To North America* (N.Y.: The New York Public Library, 1963).

You should also look at Colket and Bridgers' *Guide To Genealogical Records In The National Archives;* it has an excellent, thorough section on what records are available in these specific categories: (1) passenger arrival lists; (2) customs passenger lists; (3) customs lists of aliens; (4) immigration passenger lists. Nearly all these records are arranged by the Atlantic or Gulf of Mexico port where the immigrant's ship landed. Many gaps exist in these records; only some are indexed. Unless you know the port an ancestor entered, and about when he or she did so, you will have a great deal of searching to do. Specific details about these records are so varied and detailed, you will have to see a copy of either Lancour, or Colket and Bridgers. You can find additional help in Greenwood's *The Researcher's Guide To American Genealogy,* and in Rubincam's *Genealogical Research: Methods and Sources.*

The following table, taken from the National Archives pamphlet titled *Genealogical Records In The National Archives,* will show you generally for what years records about immigrants are available for the major port cities through which they entered (Colket and Bridgers has a much more detailed table showing many more specific port cities)

Port	Customs Passenger Lists	Immigrant Passenger Lists	Indexes
Baltimore	1820-91	1891-1909	1820-1952
Boston	1820-74, 1883-91	1891-1943	1848-91, 1902-20
New Orleans	1820-1902	1903-45	1853-1952
New York	1820-97	1897-1942	1820-46, 1897-194
Philadelphia	1800-82	1883-1945	1800-1948
Certain Minor Ports	1820-73	1893-1945	1890-1924

(Supplementing the indexes listed above is a general index to quarterly reports of arrivals at most ports except New York, 1820-74; this general index is also at the National Archives).

A *customs passenger list* normally contains the following information for each passenger: his name, age, sex, and occupation; the country from which he came; the country to which he was going; if he died in passage, the date and circumstances of his death. The *immigration passenger lists* that are more than 50 years old (those less than 50 years old are not available for reference purposes) vary in what information they contain, but usually show the place of birth and last place of residence in addition to the information found in the customs passenger lists. Some of the immigration passenger lists include the name and address of a relative in the country from which the passenger came.

Requests to have the National Archives search these records must be made on GSA Form 7111, *Order for Copies-Passenger Lists.* You must provide them with very precise data on the full name of the immigrant, his date of arrival, the ship name, and the port of entry.

Many of these records are available on microfilm; for details of what microfilms can be purchased, see the catalog, *National Archives Microfilm Publications* (Washington, D.C.: National Archives, 1974). Look under the Department of the Treasury's Records of the Bureau of the Customs-RG36; also look under the Department of Justice's Records of the Immigration and Naturalization Service-RG 85.

Finally, check the archives of the state in which you think your immigrant ancestor landed. Ask about books or lists of immigrants for that state; you might find some real help that way.

15. AMERICAN INDIAN RECORDS.

The National Archives' pamphlet, *Genealogical Records In The National Archives*, mentions these items pertaining to American Indians:

There are in the National Archives many records relating to Indians who kept their tribal status. The records, arranged by tribes, are dated chiefly 1830-1940. They include lists of Indians (chiefly Cherokee, Chickasaw, Choctaw, and Creek) who moved west during the period 1830-46; annuity pay rolls, 1841-1949; annual census rolls, 1885-1940 (available on microfilm); and Eastern Cherokee claim files, 1902-1910.

The lists normally contain the name of the head of the family, the number of persons in the family by age and sex, the description of property owned before removal (including the location of real property), and the dates of departure from the East and arrival in the West.

Annuity pay rolls (except the early ones that gave little but the names of heads of families) show the name, age and sex of each person who received payment.

The annual census rolls normally show for each person listed his Indian or English name or both (names are grouped by family), age, sex, and relationship to the head of the family and sometimes to another enrolled Indian. Occasionally on the rolls may be found supplementary information, such as names of persons who died or were born during the year. The National Archives will search the records if given the Indian's name (preferably both his English and Indian names), the name of his tribe, and the approximate date of his association with the tribe.

The Eastern Cherokee claim files usually contain the name of the applicant, his residence, the date and place of his birth, the name and age of his spouse, the names of his father and mother and of his children, and other genealogical information. For a search of the claim files, the name of the claimant (or his claim number) and his age when the claim was filed or the date of his birth are necessary. Such additional information about the claimant as his place of residence when the claim was filed, the name of his spouse, and the names of his parents or children will facilitate the search.

You should look in Colket and Bridgers, *Guide To Genealogical Records In The National Archives*, for more detailed information about these records. Also, write the Bureau of Indian Affairs, 1951 Constitution Ave., N.W., Washington, D.C. Check with the Oklahoma State Historical Society, Historical Building, Oklahoma City, Oklahoma 73105, for more recent Indian records. In addition, Filby's *American and British Genealogy and Heraldry (A Selected List of Books)*, has a good section on Indians. Finally, ask local and state libraries for the numerous books about specific tribes, and histories involving Indians generally.

Some Indian census and other records are available on microfilm. See *National Archives Microfilm Publications*, under the Department of the Interior's Records of the Bureau of Indian

Affairs - RG 75. Besides this, write for the National Archives special microfilm catalog called *The American Indian* (1972).

16. INSURANCE RECORDS.

Individual insurance companies maintain records, but what becomes of them after a certain length of time is up to that company. Write the headquarters of the company which insured your ancestor. Also, check the *Harvard Guide To American History* for these and other business histories.

Don't overlook state archives. The Virginia State Archives, for example, has the Mutual Assurance Society's records from 1796-1850 on microfilm (though unfortunately the index to these goes only to 1821).

17. LAND RECORDS.

Land records can be among the most valuable sources of information you will find, since nearly every family owns land at some time. Generally, land records mean anything pertaining to land purchases or sales, involving the transfer of land ownership from one individual to another, or from some government or official organization to an individual. Land records include patents, grants, surveys, warrants, bounty warrants, deeds, etc. (Land tax records also fit this category; see the section entitled 'Tax Records'). Let's look at these different types of records one at a time.

a. *Patents and Grants.* In colonial days, the English crown or the colonial government granted land to various individuals. Title to such land was transferred by a document called a *patent*. After the Revolutionary War, the various states and the federal government continued the practice of transferring ownership of land by documents called land *grants*. Sometimes, such land was granted in exchange for money, sometimes for military service, sometimes as headright grants (so many acres—usually 50—for each indentured servant brought over to America), sometimes if the person agreed to homestead the land for a period of time, sometimes for other reasons.

The records you might find connected with these patents or

grants are these: (1) the application or petition; (2) the warrant, or receipt for the money paid to the treasurer's office; (3) the order to survey the land; (4) the survey itself; (5) the actual grant or patent document itself, or a copy of it. These copies are often in Patent or Grant Books, which are usually indexed. Sometimes such records have been reproduced or abstracted (condensed) in published volumes. For Virginia, Nell M. Nugent wrote *Cavaliers and Pioneers (Abstracts of Virginia Land Patents and Grants 1623-1666—Vol. I, and 1666-1695—Vol. II)* (Vol. I, Baltimore, Md. Genealogical Publishing Co., 1963; Vol. II, Richmond, Va. Virginia State Library, 1977).

In a typical patent or grant you should find: the name of the person receiving the land, the county in which the land is located, the size and a description of the land, and the date of issuance of the patent or grant. The survey contains the land description, and the warrant gives the person's name and the date of issuance, along with the amount of land to which he was entitled. To find patents or grants, normally you need to know the name of the person who received the land, the county involved, and the approximate date when it was granted. Bear in mind tha .í you find a land *patent*, since these were all granted in colonial days, you may have great difficulty locating precisely the land it refers to, since boundary markers and place names often have changed or disappeared entirely. If you run into problems, ask the archives for further help.

The National Archives has some private land claims records, dating from 1789 to 1908. These involve claims to land made on the basis of grants or settlements, usually from foreign sovereigns, that took place before the United States acquired sovereignty over the land. Such lands are located in the Northwest Territory, Mississippi Territory, Louisiana, Missouri Territory, Florida, California, Arizona, Colorado, and New Mexico.

In addition, the National Archives has records of land claims dating between 1908 and 1950. Each file shows details about the person, the land, its location, and the date of land transfer. See Colket and Bridgers, *Guide To Genealogical Records In The National Archives* for further details.

b. *Bounty Warrants.* Bounty warrants are documents relating to public land given to soldiers who served in various wars. Some of this land was awarded by the state in whose army the soldier served; much of it after 1783 was granted by the United States Government.

The Virginia State Archives, for example, has French and Indian War Bounty Certificates. For service in this war, the amount of bounty land a soldier could receive depended on his length of service and rank: a field officer was entitled to 5,000 acres, a private to 50 acres. State archives and state libraries often have records pertaining to bounty warrants, as well as to the categories discussed above, patents and grants.

The records connected with bounty warrants which might help you are applications for bounty warrants, land office military certificates (which are often indexed), and the bounty warrants themselves (which are themselves often indexed). Provided you know the name of the soldier, the warrant can tell you his rank, the amount of land he was due, and possibly other information. This can lead you to the actual grant or patent itself that will describe the location, dimensions, and other details of the land; or, it might lead you to the appropriate county records, which would yield the same information.

The National Archives also has bounty land warrants and applications for them, dating 1775-1855, dealing with the Revolutionary War and with later wars. These bounty land warrants, according to Colket and Bridgers, contain such information as the name, age, residence, military or naval unit, and period of service of the veteran, and the name, age, and place of residence of the widow or other claimant. If the application was approved, the file also shows the warrant number, the number of acres granted, the date issued, and, where appropriate, the name of the assignee. Some of these records (from 1800-1900) have been microfilmed. See the catalog titled *National Archives Microfilm Publications*, under 'Other Agencies,' Records of the Veterans' Administration - RG 15.

A reference book that may help you understand this whole subject is Thomas Donaldson's *The Public Domain* (Washington, D.C.: Government Printing Office, 1884). See also Roy M.

Robbins' *Our Landed Heritage: The Public Domain 1776-1936* (London, Neb.: University of Nebraska Press, 1962).

c. *Deeds.* Deed books are an excellent source of genealogical information. Deed books can be found among county records, or in state archives. Consult them in the archives, because your ancestors may have owned land in more than one county.

Most deeds have been photostated, and these photostats bound into books available for your use. Each volume pertains to a specific county or city, and to a particular span of years. For instance, a deed book might be entitled *Southampton County Deed Book No. 4, 1855-1860.* Usually, each volume is indexed, although these indexes can be incomplete. Also, many deed records have been microfilmed, and you can use them that way if you like.

Besides the deed itself, various kinds of records connected with buying and selling of land may be helpful to you: bills of sale, powers of attorney, antenuptual contract (an agreement made at the time of a second marriage, designating property settlements for previously owned land), and so on.

" MY GREAT-GRANDFATHER OWNED SOME SCENIC PROPERTY IN THE COUNTRY"

Land descriptions have units of measurement in them that might be mysterious to you; here is a list of such terms and their meanings:

Acre—43,560 square feet.

Chain—66 feet, or 22 yards (100 links).

Furlong—660 feet, or 220 yards (10 chains).

Link—7.92 inches (25 links equal a rod, 100 links equal a chain).

Mile—5,280 feet (80 chains, 32 rods, or 8 furlongs).

Perch—5½ yards, or 16½ feet (sometimes this is called a rod or pole).

Rood—Can vary in meaning from one rod to about 8 feet; sometimes means ¼ of an acre.

Whenever you find a deed for land owned by your ancestor, copy down all the information in it; you can never tell when you might want to visit that property, and need the specifics. Also, the deed might reveal details about family relationships or other information.

If you want to find out something about the buildings on the property, whether or not they are still standing, check among city records in what are called Mechanics' Lien Books.

Finally, remember that you might find among family papers an unrecorded deed. Record-keeping was not as thorough in the old days, so the clerk simply might have forgotten to record it.

18. MANUSCRIPT COLLECTIONS.

A useful guide to various American manuscript collections is the *National Union Catalog of Manuscript Collections* (Washington, D.C.: Library of Congress, 1959). In this are descriptions of more than 27,000 manuscript collections in over 800 locations.

For manuscripts in a particular state, besides checking the state library and archives, look through the holdings of various private and public historical societies, museums, etc.

19. MAPS.

The further back you trace, the more likely you are to run

into the problem of changed place names. This problem can involve names of states, counties, towns or cities, creeks, mountains, or any other landmark. One of the best aids you can find is a map that dates within a half-century or so of the years you're researching.

Old land-ownership maps might be of great help to you. The Library of Congress has a large collection of these (1,449 maps from 1,041 U.S. counties, about ⅓ of all American counties). Details about these maps can be found in a booklet by Richard W. Stephenson, *Land-Ownership Maps* (Washington, D.C.: Library of Congress, 1967), for sale by the Library of Congress. Most of the maps he lists date from the 19th Century, and the Library of Congress will send you a photostatic copy of the ones you need for a reasonable fee.

Besides those in the Library of Congress, every major library or archives should have originals or copies of some old maps. Explain your problem to the archivist or librarian, and they will tell you whether or not their map holdings might help you.

These sources may be useful as well:

a. *Bullinger's Postal and Shippers Guide for the United States and Canada* (Westwood, N.J.: Bullinger's Guides, Inc., published annually since 1897).

b. The U.S. Post Office Department's *United States Directory of Post Offices* (published annually; of course, it lists only those towns, etc., that have post offices).

c. *Gazetteers*—There are several of these, such as the *Columbia-Lippincott Gazetteer of the World.* These list place names alphabetically.

d. *Atlases.* Especially useful are historical atlases. You should be able to find one or more of these in your local library.

e. *Old city or county maps.* Ask the library or chamber of commerce if any of these are available, and where they can be found.

20. MARRIAGE RECORDS.

You may find records of marriages in any of several sources:

a. *Family Bibles.*

b. *Marriage Bonds*. These are records of amounts of money posted with the state in case a lawful obstruction to the proposed marriage occurred. Attached is usually the fiancee's written consent, the name of the proposed spouse, and another male name, probably the co-signer of the bond, along with the date the bond was paid. For many counties these have been compiled in books or lists, and arranged in alphabetical order.

c. *Indexes* to marriages in various publications. For example, the Baptist newspaper, *Religious Herald*, has compiled an index of marriage notices in its pages from 1828-1938. The *Southern Churchman* has an index covering 1835-1941. You will no doubt find others for different states and areas; ask about them at your state library or archives.

d. *Ministers' Returns*. These are detailed reports ministers filed with state officials telling of the marriages they performed.

e. *Court Records*. Sometimes marriage records formed part of official court records. Most such records would be on microfilm.

f. *Alphabetical listings* of marriages for a whole state. Often these are in book form. Check with your state library or archives.

g. *Church Records*. Before states began keeping official records, information about marriages was often kept by churches (in Virginia, for instance, by the Episcopal Church located in each parish). Thus, the further back in time you go, the more likely you will have to depend either on family records or church records. See the separate section on church records in this chapter for how and where to locate them.

Finally, two pamphlets that might help you are *Where to Write for Marriage Records*, and *Where to Write for Divorce Records*. Both are available for 15 cents each from The Superintendent of Documents, U.S. Government Printing Office, Washington, D.C. 20402.

21. MILITARY SERVICE RECORDS.

Military records are invaluable as a source of information

about male ancestors, and occasionally about females. Military records normally are found only at two levels of authority: state and national. They will be on deposit mainly in one of three places: the state archives (or state library), the National Archives or one of the regional Federal Records Centers, or the appropriate branch of the service (Army, Navy, Air Force, Marines).

Don't assume you must write the National Archives for everything; your state archives may well have quite a lot of military information on its citizens. Many times, records pertaining to Colonial Wars, the Revolutionary War, the War of 1812, and the Civil War can be found in book form or on microfilm at the state library or archives. For instance, H. J. Eckenrode wrote a book called *List of the Colonial Soldiers of Virginia*, as well as another one titled *List of the Revolutionary Soldiers of Virginia*. Each of the states should have similar books for its soldiers. For a list of some of them, see Val Greenwood's *The Researcher's Guide To American Genealogy*, pages 431 and following.

Especially in older wars, soldiers served under several possible jurisdictions, so it depends on which one they were under as to where their service records would be located. During the Revolutionary War, for instance, a Virginia soldier could have served in one of four different levels of service:

a. *Continental Troops.* Virginia furnished 15 Regiments to the Continental Army. Records pertaining to these would be at the National Archives.

b. *State Line Troops.* These included 3 regular infantry regiments, an artillery regiment, a cavalry regiment, the 'State Garrison Regiment,' two regiments in Illinois, 'Convention Troops' guarding prisoners from the battle of Saratoga that were kept near Charlottesville, and finally, Dabney's State Legion. Those records that still exist concerning these troops would be found in the Virginia State Archives. The same principle would apply to state troops from the other states as well.

c. *Militia Troops.* Records concerning these would be found at the state level.

d. *Navy*. Records about these troops would be found in the National Archives.

What military records are housed in the National Archives itself? Colket and Bridgers mention the following:

United States military records dated 1775-1912, with a few as late as 1917 and records of burials to 1939. They are incomplete because fires in Washington, D.C. on November 8, 1800, and August 24, 1814, destroyed many Revolutionary War and other records. The existing records include military service records of the Regular Army, 1784-1917, but chiefly 1800-1912; military records of the Revolutionary War, 1775-83; military service records of volunteer organizations of the War of 1812, Mexican War, Civil War, Spanish-American War, and other periods of military operations, 1784-1903; miscellaneous military records, 1784-1815; Civil War draft records, 1863-65; burial records of soldiers, 1775-1939; and records of births, marriages, and civilian deaths at army posts, 1884-1912. They also have records concerning the Confederate States of America.

Information found in these records varies. If you know the name of the soldier, and the state from which he served, you should learn from these records at least the soldier's basic military information: rank, length of service, where he served, etc. Sometimes, the records also show next of kin, date of birth, names of wife and children, and other personal information. Colket and Bridger's *Guide To Genealogical Records In The National Archives* has a detailed rundown on what types of information the records of each war or period show, as well as what records are available. A more summary treatment is in the pamphlet, *Military Service Records In The National Archives*, (Pamphlet No. 8). Write for your free copy from the Publication Sales Branch (NATS), National Archives (GSA), Washington, D.C. 20408.

The National Archives will search the registers of enlistments or the compiled military service records of an individual soldier, if you submit a request on GSA Form 6751, *Order for Copies—Veterans Records* (these forms are available from the

National Archives). Whenever information is desired about military service—either Union or Confederate—in the Civil War, the name of the state from which the soldier served must be given. If a compiled military service record or an entry in an enlistment register is found, photocopies of the records will be supplied (for a fee) if the service was rendered more than 75 years ago; records of more recent service are subject to restrictions imposed by the Department of Defense. If the records in the National Archives relate to service within the past 75 years, a written statement of the service of the soldier will be sent free of charge.

Requests for information about Army officers separated after 1916 and Army enlisted personnel separated after 1912 should be made on Standard Form 180, *Request Pertaining To Military Records*, and sent to Military Personnel Records (GSA), 9700 Page Boulevard, St. Louis, Missouri 63132.

Of particular help with World War I veterans (since their records are not yet open to the public) are the Selective Service Cards of World War I. These show the place of birth, age, address, next of kin, and marital status of all men of draft age in the United States in 1918. These cards are housed at the Federal Records Center, 1557 St. Joseph Ave., East Point, Georgia 30344. The personnel there will search these cards for a small charge, if you give them the city and the state where the man registered.

The National Archives also has records relating to American naval and marine service in the Revolutionary War (1775-83), and in the U.S. Navy (for officers, 1798-1902, and enlisted men, 1798-1885), as well as in the U.S. Marine Corps (1798-1895). In addition, they have records for some people who served in the Confederate Navy and Marine Corps (1861-65).

These records, particularly the naval ones, are sketchy, especially in the early years. If you do find your man in them, the records will show basic information about his military service. If you write the National Archives about someone in these services, send his name, the name of the war in which he served or the dates of his service. For a Navy enlisted man, you need to give at least one of the ships on which he served (with approximate dates). Without the name of the ship, you would have to search reel-by-reel through the microfilm.

Requests for information about Navy officers separated since 1902, Navy enlisted men separated since 1885, and Marine Corps officers and enlisted men separated after 1895 should be made on Standard Form 180, *Request Pertaining to Military Records*. Send these to Military Personnel Records (GSA), 9700 Page Boulevard, St. Louis, Missouri 63132.

The National Archives also has records of Coast Guard personnel, and records of predecessor organizations. The Coast Guard was created in 1915 out of the older Revenue Cutter Service and Life-Saving Service. The Revenue Cutter Service dates back to 1791. If you write the National Archives about a member of any of these services, give as complete information about him as you can, including the name of the vessel on which he served, if possible.

"COUSIN BEN WAS ON GENERAL WASHINGTON'S STAFF!"

Many military records and indexes to them are available for purchase on microfilm. To see the list of these look under 'Department of War' in the catalog called *National Archives Microfilm Publications*.

22. MINUTE BOOKS.

Minute books are records kept by county governments which may also be of some help. Look for them either in the county itself, or in the state archives or state library.

23. MISCELLANEOUS POSSIBILITIES.

Besides the other records suggested in this chapter, you might try these possibilities:

a. Agricultural Society records (for instance, records of the Grange).

b. Labor Union records.

c. Lawyer's records.

d. Business records.

e. County histories.

f. Employment records.

g. Ethnic or Ethnic Society records, such as records of the Polish Club, the German Singing Club, etc.

h. Hospital records.

i. Records of Justices of the Peace.

j. Police records.

k. Medical records.

l. Voting lists.

m. Bank records.

n. Notary Public records.

o. Others that perhaps only you could think of.

24. NEWSPAPERS.

Newspapers are somewhat difficult to use, because most of

them have no name index. You must go through every page to find anything. They can be helpful in some ways, though. Within a week after a person's death, his or her obituary might appear in the paper. Sometimes newspapers devoted a regular space to deaths of veterans of various wars, such as the Revolutionary and Civil Wars. For example, the Richmond, Virginia, *Enquirer* carried death notices of Revolutionary War soldiers; the Virginia State Archives has copies of these.

Sometimes, newspapers carried genealogical articles. The *Boston Evening Transcript* had an especially good series of these, beginning in 1876 and appearing for the next half-century. In many cases where such genealogical articles appear in newspapers, however, their quality is questionable, since you have no way of knowing who worked on the material, what sources they used, etc.

You might also find in newspapers such things as birth announcements, marriage notices, or perhaps some article about your relatives. Occasionally, such items are indexed. The American Antiquarian Society of Worcester, Massachusetts, has indexed all marriage and death notices from the Boston newspaper, *Columbia Centinel*, between 1784 and 1840. Always check with the state library or state archives to find out if any such indexing has been done and where the indexes can be found.

If you have run out of other possibilities, turn to newspapers, but expect to have to spend many long hours in front of a microfilm reader to find even the slightest information in them. Still, if newspapers are all you have, they can be of tremendous help. As mentioned earlier, I found a newspaper article describing a court trial, which provided the key to what I needed, when I had all but given up since the court records themselves had been burned.

Where can you find old newspapers? Try newspaper companies that are still in business; ask to see their old copies, or, better yet, ask if they have them on microfilm, or if they have turned their old issues over to a library or archives. Then, try the public library. Ask also at the state library, as well as any local or regional historical society. Wherever you find them, if you have a choice between seeing the originals and getting microfilm copies, use the microfilm. Newsprint, especially that used since 1900, darkens and rapidly becomes brittle with age.

On the other hand, older newspapers printed on high rag content paper are often in better shape than those printed since 1900. In some cases, libraries or other depositories will have newspapers as far back as colonial days. For instance, copies of the *Virginia Gazette* dating from the Colonial period still exist.

For general help, try these three volumes: (1) Clarence S. Brigham, *History and Bibliography of American Newspapers, 1690-1820* (Hamden, Conn.: Shoe String Press, 1962, 2 volumes); (2) Winifred Gregory, ed., *American Newspapers 1821-1936, A Union List of Files Available In The United States and Canada* (N.Y.: H. W. Wilson Co., 1937); (3) To find newspapers currently printed, try the *Ayer Directory of Newspapers and Periodicals* (Philadelphia, Pa.: N. W. Ayer & Sons, printed annually). Inquire also about the Library of Congress's excellent newspaper collection, with some copies dating before the Revolution.

25. PASSPORT APPLICATIONS.

The National Archives has passport applications received by the Department of State, with related records, dating from 1791-1905. Passports were not required of U.S. citizens traveling abroad (except for part of the Civil War) until the First World War. Still, many people got passports as added identification and security.

According to Colket and Bridgers, such applications (especially after the Civil War):

usually contain the name, signature, place of residence, age, and personal description of the applicant; the names or number of persons in his family intending to travel with him; the date; and, where appropriate, the date and court of naturalization. It sometimes contains the exact date and place of birth of the applicant and of his wife and minor children accompanying him, if any; and, if the applicant was a naturalized citizen, the date and port of his arrival in the United

States and the name of the vessel on which he arrived.

The use of these records is restricted. Persons wishing to confirm age or citizenship from these records that are less than 75 years old should write to the Passport Office, Department of State, Washington, D.C.

For passport records older than 75 years, write the National Archives, giving them the basic information, dates, etc., that you have.

26. PENSION RECORDS.

Related to military service records are state and federal military pension records. Usually, each state archives has lists or books of these for that state. The Virginia State Archives, for instance, has a number of volumes containing abstracts of Virginia pensions for the Revolution, the War of 1812, and the Indian Wars. In addition, it has volumes of Revolutionary War Pension Applicants. (All these of course pertain to state pensions). In some states, pensions were awarded by the legislature; for them you would have to check the index to the legislative records.

The National Archives has many federal pension records relating to the veteran himself, to his widow, and to his heirs. Colket and Bridgers describe the National Archives' holdings of pension records as follows:

'They relate to military, naval, and marine service performed between 1775 and 1934, exclusive of Confederate and World War I service. The benefits included pensions, rights to land, special naval awards, and domiciliary care. The records consist of pension application records, pension payment records, bounty-land warrant application records, claims files for special naval awards, and records of Federal homes.'

A number of pension records, and indexes to them, are available on microfilm; see the National Archives microfilm publications catalog, under 'Other Agencies,' Records of the Veterans Administration RG-15, or inquire directly to the National Archives.

27. PETITIONS.

All colonies before, and many states since the Revolution, permitted citizens to petition the Colonial or State Government concerning various needs. An individual or a group might submit a petition on such subjects as: hardships due to war wounds, war widows asking support, claims for wagons or goods impressed by troops, claims for bounty lands, incorporation of towns, establishment of banks, ferries, mills, canals, to divide counties, to prevent hogs, cattle, etc., from running wild in city streets, worthlessness of the paper currency, against certain taxes, for a divorce, concerning various aspects of religion, for or against slavery, etc.

In Virginia, these petitions are organized by counties or independent cities. Other states may organize them by legislative session. Although petitions sound like a good genealogical source, they are very difficult to use. No name index to the people who signed them exists; signatures are not in alphabetical order. Thus, you would need to search page by page to find an ancestor's name, and even if you did locate the name, all it would tell you is that he lived in a certain county or city and was interested in the subject mentioned in the petition. Sometimes, you might find your ancestor's signature. Often, though, signatures were merely an X, with the person's name printed beside the X by someone else; or the signatures would have all been written on the petition itself by the same person who had permission to do so from the people whose names he signed.

Use petitions only if absolutely no other source for finding your ancestor exists. There are more efficient methods of tracing your family tree.

28. PHONE BOOKS.

Phone books are not as useful as city directories, but they can help. Make a habit of checking the phone book of whatever city you are in for people of the names you are interested in. Take down their names, addresses, and phone numbers. Write or call them, explain what you're doing, and ask them to give you what family information they can. In the case of more common families (Smith, Brown, etc.), you could waste a lot of time this way. For more unfamiliar family names, it might help.

Also, you can check old phone books to see whether or not your ancestor lived there at that time (bear in mind he might have moved away right after the phone book came out; or, he could have moved there shortly after the phone book was published; thus, he could have lived there less or more time than the phone book indicates).

The Library of Congress has an extensive collection of phone books, most of them current ones. Also try your state library, local libraries, the phone company, local college or university libraries and alumnae offices, as well as local historical societies.

29. PUBLIC SERVICE CLAIMS.

These are claims by private individuals asking to be repaid for some service rendered to the state government, or for some item of property (wagon, cow, pig, etc.) they provided the army or the state government. At least in Virginia, Public Service Claims are filed alphabetically. Ask at your state archives to see whether or not your state has such records.

30. SCHOOL RECORDS.

Write the State Department of Education in the state where your ancestor lived; they should be able to tell you something about what records are available, and where they can be found. Sometimes, you can find old public school records in the state archives.

If your ancestor went to a particular college or university, write that school and ask them if they still have the records on him or her. Most colleges or universities have undergone name changes through the years, but the records stay in that institution regardless. For example, Washington and Lee University in Lexington, Virginia, was known as Washington College before Robert E. Lee served as its president. Washington College was originally Liberty Hall Academy. Thus, if you learn that your great-great grandfather graduated from Washington College in

Lexington, Virginia, ask yourself what college in Lexington would probably be the successor institution; then write them. They will tell you if you guessed right.

On the other hand, many colleges have closed. Their records could wind up almost anywhere. Try writing a nearby college first; sometimes defunct colleges pass their records on to neighboring colleges. Also write the Chamber of Commerce of the city where the college used to operate. If they can't help you, maybe they can give you suggestions of where to look further.

31. CALENDARS OF STATE PAPERS.

Most states have published the official correspondence to and from their past governors, along with certain other papers. These are usually published in a number of volumes, and each volume is indexed. They can be found in various libraries, and in the state library or archives. If your ancestor had any business with the state government, his name might appear in one or more of these volumes. If other sources yield nothing, try these calendars.

32. TAX RECORDS.

This is one kind of record that everyone living in any given area has to pay. You will be examining mainly two types of taxes, land taxes, and personal property taxes. Not everyone owned land, but everyone owns some personal property. Unfortunately, though, only the name of the person charged with paying the tax (usually the head of the household) is normally found in the tax records. Let's look at the two main types of taxes:

a. *Land Taxes.* As with deeds and wills, you usually find land tax records either on microfilm or photostated and bound in large books. These books are arranged by county, by year, and by the name of the tax commissioner. Land tax records are rarely indexed; instead they are arranged alphabetically in each tax commissioner's list (bear in mind a single county may have more than one commissioner, hence more than one alphabetical list may be in one tax book.)

Land tax records may show all or part of the following information: number of lots owned, yearly rent of lots (if rented), quantity of land (in acres), value of land, total number of lots and land along with their money value, value of buildings on the property, tax amount, residence name, town name, number of town lots, sometimes location of the land (for instance, distance and bearing from the courthouse), alterations during the preceding year, etc.

In states which have independent cities, such as Virginia, tax records are filed alphabetically by county, then this list is followed by an alphabetical list of cities. Look for land tax records either in counties or in the state archives.

b. *Personal Property Taxes.* As with land taxes, personal property taxes are arranged alphabetically by commissioner, by county, and by year. Information given in them may concern how many of the following a person had: billiard tables, stud horses, wheels (on carriages), slaves, ordinary (that is, a tavern-lodging house) license, cattle, indentured white servants, bureaus and desks, etc.

Another category that to some degree overlaps personal property taxes is called *tithables.* These are lists of taxable people, including sons above 16, tithable blacks, and certain tithable items such as carriages, etc.

Although the next type is not a tax record, this is a good place to mention it. I refer to *rent rolls,* which recorded rents collected for absentee owners of land, and for others.

Sometimes you will find some information in miscellaneous auditors' records and miscellaneous tax papers. Also, some records of insolvents, delinquent lands, etc., exist. You will probably have to ask for these at the archives desk. All these tax records can be seen either in the counties themselves, or in the state archives.

33. WILLS.

Wills, as with deeds, are available in state archives, often both on microfilm and in bound photostat volumes. The bound volumes and the microfilm are arranged by county of probate, and by blocks of years (example: 1830-1840). Each volume or reel is indexed.

For at least some states, private individuals have compiled wills or references to them in book form. For Virginia, see Clayton Torrence's *Virginia Wills and Administrations 1632-1800* (Richmond, Va.: The William Byrd Press, 1931). Such books as Torrence missed some wills; ask at the archives desk for suggestions of ways to find wills such volumes missed.

Wills can be very valuable to you. To begin with, they usually list the living members of the family (you must locate deceased members from other sources, such as property tax records, census records, etc.). Then, wills often give other family information, such as property or possessions owned by the deceased.

To obtain copies of wills, write the appropriate county, or the state archives, giving them the name of the person whose will you desire, his or her date of death, and the county of probate. If you don't know the date of death, give an educated guess. For a small fee, the archives or the county clerk will send you a photostat copy of the will itself.

Some people died without a will, which is called in legal language, intestate. In such cases, that county's court appoints an administrator to oversee the distribution of the property and care for the heirs. In county records, administrators' accounts and reports are indexed according to the deceased's name. You might also find guardians' records or guardians' bonds, if the court had to appoint a guardian for the minor children.

If you are copying a will yourself, be sure to take down every item of specific information, no matter how unimportant it may seem. You can ignore the flowery legal language usually, but get the facts down carefully: get all names, descriptions of people or property, relationships mentioned, and so on. If you can afford it, have the library or archives Xerox or photostat the will for you. When they mail it to you, code it for that person (M3F, etc.), and file it in the appropriate place.

SUMMARY OF PRIMARY SOURCES.

In this chapter I have discussed nearly all of the primary

sources you will have occasion to use in your search. Some of them will be more valuable to you than others. Read through my descriptions of each type, and make a list of those you think will help your particular search most of all. Look at those records in the appropriate depository. Then, if they have not given you the information you need, try the sources you did not list. The point is that primary sources are the best sources of all in most cases. Keep searching through them until you find the information you need. Don't give up; enjoy what you're learning as you search through different kinds of records. You'll learn a surprising amount about your country and your family as you do.

" MY FAMILY MOVED WEST FOR FEAR
OF BEING PENNED IN ?"

Chapter Three
Secondary Sources

Secondary sources do not contain the actual primary records themselves, but supposedly have been written based on the primary records. The main problem with secondary sources is that you cannot be certain of their quality. They might be inaccurate, biased, or incomplete. As much as possible, check their quality by examining for yourself the primary records on which they are based.

Here are the main secondary sources you will use:

1. BIOGRAPHIES.

Biographies are a category of almost endless possibilities. Some kind of biographical information is published about many people, especially the prominent, but many times the common people as well. Where can you find such biographies?

First, try libraries. Look in the reference section, for such volumes as: *Who's Who; Who Was Who; Biographical Encyclopedia of the World; The New York Times Biographical Edition; The McGraw-Hill Encyclopedia of World Biography; Dictionary of American Biography; Who Was Who In America; Who's Who In The South And Southwest; Current Biography Yearbook;* etc.

Besides these, try the *New York Times Index* in your local library. Also look through the *Harvard Guide To American History* (it has more than 100 pages of references to biographical books). Search the card files at your local library, and the state library and archives. As an example, the Virginia State Archives has an interesting collection of information on lesser known people from Virginia, compiled by S. Bassett French. I'm certain other state libraries or archives have similar files. Ask them.

2. GENEALOGICAL NOTES AND CHARTS.

In chapter one, I mentioned published genealogies. Besides published ones, you can usually find in state archives or state libraries (not to mention local libraries or historical societies, etc.) copies of genealogical notes or charts deposited there by the family member who compiled them, or by a genealogist. Ask the desk personnel about this possibility when you visit the depository. Remember, though, these genealogies may or may not be very accurate.

3. LOCAL HISTORIES.

Local histories, as with genealogical notes, can be of fine or of poor quality. In either case, they can provide you with extremely valuable information or clues which will help your search. Sometimes local histories contain accounts by local people that will give you information you could get in no other way.

The *Harvard Guide to American History* has an excellent list of books on local history, state historical publications, etc. In addition, look at *U.S. Local Histories In The Library of Congress: A Bibliography* (Baltimore, Md.: Magna Carta Book Co., 4 volumes). This latter one would be good to recommend to your local library for addition to its collection.

Finally, look in local libraries in the area you are researching, as well as in the state library of that state.

4. NEWSPAPERS.

Newspapers can be both primary and secondary sources, so I list them in both categories.

As I said earlier, some newspapers (for example the Richmond, Virginia *Times-Dispatch* from 9 August 1903 to 3 June 1917), contain genealogical articles about different families.

Furthermore, your ancestor may have been mentioned in a newspaper article. Newspapers, especially local ones, often run stories or even a series about local history. In any of these you might find some information or clues that could help you. Remember, though, that newspaper reporters sometimes are more interested in getting a story out than checking all the historical sources, so their articles may have inaccuracies. Check behind them yourself as much as you can.

With some exceptions, most newspapers are not indexed. However, you will find name indexes to articles in the *New York Times* on file in most local libraries.

5. PERIODICALS.

Genealogical periodicals usually contain advertisements by individuals researching their family, offering to trade information, etc.; they list professional genealogists, companies that can help, bookstores, books, articles, etc. Try to get your local library to subscribe to at least one such periodical.

Lists of them can be found in Mary K. Meyer's *Directory Of Genealogical Societies In The U.S.A. and Canada with an appended list of Independent Genealogical Periodicals* (Pasadena, Md.: M.K. Meyer, Rt. 10, Box 138-A, Pasadena, Md., 1976). Her lists of periodicals are organized by state, then by city. She gives addresses, cost, etc.

Historical society periodicals, or magazines of state history can be helpful to you as well.

Chapter Four
Common Problems and How to Deal with Them

1. VARIATIONS IN SPELLING OF FAMILY NAMES.

Whatever notions you may have about the purity of the spelling of your family name, put them away. Especially before the 20th Century, if your ancestors could read and write (and not many people could), most of them spelled words poorly. Usually, words would be spelled the way they sounded to the writer. I've seen a letter by Thomas Jefferson in which he spelled 'Berkeley' as 'Barkley.' That was probably the way he pronounced it.

In the mountains of Virginia, in my wife's home area, live a number of people named Cockram. This name was originally Cockerham. Since most people pronounced it Cockram, that's the way most people spelled it. Some even rendered it Cochrane.

In the spelling of my own family name, I have found quite a few variations, and I list them here to show you the variations you may run into with your own name: Peteet, Potteet, Potest, Poteet, Pateet, Patteet, Putteet, Poteete, Peeteet, Peetett, Potteete, Poteett, Potete, Peteate, Peteete, Potent, Pettet, Poteat. I suspect (but have not yet proven) that the various names like Pettit are related to us, since the original name for all of these was probably Petit, which means *little* in French.

When looking up your own relatives in the records, keep an open mind. You might even make a list of possible spelling variations (use your imagination). You need to be aware of this problem because many records have alphabetical name indexes. If you look under the spelling you use today, you may miss your ancestor entirely.

Here is a fairly typical example of poor spelling in older documents, this from a Virginia petition of 1776:

> The humble petition of Charles Henly sheweth that he Humble begith your pardons A Thousand times hopeing that you will have marcy pety and Compartion on a pore man which I have bin som time ago Confused by som part of the scripter - Romans 13 sense Independentcey is declared and A governour Anounted my desier is to serve my Country and the powers that is in it: my Contions is Content to seport and defend my Country for the sake of my wife and Children as long as I shall liv and willin To take the: oath to the United States of the Amarykey.

Besides spelling problems, you may find that the family name has been changed entirely or translated when your ancestor first came to America. If he was a German named Schwartz (*black*), he might become Mr. Black. Kowalski might become Kowal, Petropopovich might become Peters, or Smith, etc. Changes were made in first names as well. So as you come to immigrant ancestors, watch for this possibility.

2. SIMILAR FIRST NAMES.

The same first names often appear in different generations of a family. In one of my lines, the name Mary appears in several generations. Be alert to this potential problem. You can confuse your records if you haven't recorded which one you're talking about.

This is where the code I suggested will help (3FM, etc.). Even though two people's names may be the same, they will have different codes to help you keep them straight.

In some cases, one child might receive a dead brother or sis-

ter's name. The parents might do this to honor the child who died, or else to perpetuate the name. If birthdates of children are spread over a fairly long time—say 25 years—the husband may have remarried after his wife's death. Many women died in childbirth, especially before the 20th Century. Also, since children were born on an average of every two years, if you run across a gap in that pattern, suspect a stillborn child, or one who died young (though of course this may not be the case).

Be alert to the possibility of nicknames, too; the same person might be called by a given name and by a nickname, leading you to mistakenly conclude you've found two different people.

So, keep the generations straight, by assigning a code to every individual on whom you're working. You might even want to put the death date beside the name as extra help: John Jones, 3FMF, d. 1856.

3. WORDS THAT MAY MISLEAD YOU ABOUT RELATIONSHIPS BETWEEN PEOPLE.

Words that mean one type of blood relationship between people today may have meant something quite different in earlier centuries. Here are the most common such cases:

a. *Junior (Jr.) or Senior (Sr.).* This might mean an uncle-nephew relationship rather than father-son. It also may mean a cousin. Since before the last century there were few middle names, calling someone Junior and Senior was a convenient way of distinguishing between the elder and the younger. Sometimes families might have more than two generations with the same name; the eldest might be called Senior, the next younger, Junior, the next the Third, and so on. When Senior died, each one might move up a notch. So, be careful what you conclude from these terms.

b. *Mister (Mr.) or Missus (Mrs.).* During the 1600's and 1700's, these titles often were used only for citizens of higher social rank, such as ministers, prominent landowners, and the like. Those who fell a notch below this on the social scale were sometimes called *Goodman* or *Goodwife (Goody).*

c. *Sister or Brother.* These might mean any one of these things: a blood brother or sister, a sister-in-law or brother-in-law, or they might be used in the Christian sense of a brother or sister in Christ (that is, a fellow Christian).

d. *Cousin.* This term was used extremely loosely, especially before 1750. It could mean first cousin, or one further removed, or even a nephew or niece.

e. *Nephew or Niece.* These words usually mean what they say, but occasionally they can mean grandchild; this meaning does not occur very frequently, however.

f. The phrase, *my present wife,* or, *my now wife,* was merely an expression, and may or may not mean the man had a previous wife.

g. *Natural Child.* This means legitimate child. Illegitimate children were indicated in obvious ways such as *bastard, base child,,* etc. Further, if you run across the term *alias*, as in Robert Brown *alias* Cooke, it means he is probably illegitimate, the Brown referring to the name of the man who was probably his father, the Cooke referring to his mother's name. At times, *alias* meant the child was adopted, or that he took both his father's and mother's names (an echo of the English practice of hyphenated names, such as the former British Prime Minister Henry Campbell-Bannerman).

4. SKELETONS IN THE FAMILY TREE.

I have talked with a professional genealogist who admitted falsifying the family tree of a prominent Virginia family (at their request) to cover up a bastard child. Some people only want to find prominent, moral, hard-working people in their family tree. I'm convinced that no family on earth fits that description. If you think about the members of your family living right now, you will surely find both good and bad people. It was the same in earlier centuries.

"GRANDFATHER WAS THE FIRST MANUFACTURER IN THIS AREA?"

Then, too, you need to remember that in frontier days (whether the frontier was the Appalachian Mountains in 1775, or Oregon or California in 1870), many areas had no preacher to perform marriages. A man and woman who wanted to marry would be forced to live together without being legally married sometimes for a year or more, until a preacher appeared on the scene. I have read a number of petitions by 18th Century Virginians who urged the Virginia legislature to send preachers to perform weddings for couples who were living together. Naturally, any children born before the preacher got there would be technically illegitimate, but would be legitimized when the mother and father were married.

Don't be afraid of bastards, horse thieves, etc. We all have them in our families. If you are even partly of English ancestry, you no doubt have Anglo-Saxon blood in you. Did you know that the tribes called Angles and Saxons were cannibals for at least part of their history? So, all of us have questionable ancestors at some point.

5. OLD HANDWRITING.

I spent a year working with Virginia legislative petitions, most of which dated from 1740 to 1860. I know from experience that the handwriting from these years, as well as earlier, can be hard to read. One of the most frequently-met handwriting problems is the use of the old-style S, that resembles a modern lower-case handwritten f. You'll also run into all sorts of abbreviations; most of these refer to legal terms, such as admin^r for administrator, etc. A few of them are unfamiliar, such as *viz.* (namely), and Y^e (the). Besides these problems, the language people used in earlier centuries was more formal and flourishing than what we use today. Here is an example:

To the Honourable the Speaker and Gentlemen of the House of Delegates, Sundry inhabitants of the Frontiers of Virginia beg leave humbly to represent—That your memorialists have generally been inhabitants of the western extremities of this State for a Considerable course of time. That during a Succession of twenty five years and upwards it is well known, few seasons have passed without incursion from the Savage Natives, residing on the northwest side of the Ohio.

(Notice in this example, from a Virginia Legislative Petition of Nov. 27, 1780, the frequent use of capital letters in odd places that is so typical of older documents).

If you run into problems with the handwriting that you can't solve, simply ask the archivist or librarian for help. A book that should help you further is Kay Kirkham's *How To Read The Handwriting and Records of Early America* (Salt Lake City, Utah: Kay Publishing Co., 1961).

You may run across a signature affixed to a document written in this form:

His
John   X   Hamlin
Mark

This was done when a man or woman could not write (or was too sick to do so, or their name was being signed for them with their permission, since they couldn't be present). Most often, though, it meant the signer could not write his name. Illiteracy was nothing to be ashamed of in previous centuries; in fact, it was quite common because formal schooling was not widespread.

6. INDENTURED SERVANTS.

If an ancestor came over during the 1600's or early 1700's, he or she may have come as an indentured servant. This category, which applies only to whites, not to other races, grew out of the needs of the times. Many people wanted to come to the American colonies, but had no money. One way to pay for their trans-Atlantic passage was through entering into an indenture agreement with someone already in one of the 13 colonies. As an example, examine with me an indenture agreement between John Hampton, who owned a farm in Virginia, and Samuel Leftwich of London, England, who wanted to come to Virginia. Hampton would agree to pay the cost of Leftwich's ship passage from England to Virginia. In exchange, Leftwich would agree to serve Hampton for a specified period, usually from four to seven years. Both men would sign the indenture agreement containing the terms.

Those who became indentured servants came mainly from those too poor to pay their own way. Among them were men and women, boys and girls. Occasionally, apprentices came over under an indenture agreement. Some men and women who came as indentured servants were convicts, 'jaile birds' as one 1671 law called them.

Finding an indenture agreement for your ancestor would be difficult, for not many have survived. If you should come across one, though, it might be very helpful. I have seen one that mentioned the place the indentured servant came from in England and what his occupation was. If you trace your family back to an ancestor who came over to America, you'll find that one of the hardest things to find out is exactly the town, city, etc., he or she came from. An indenture agreement could help greatly. They might be found anywhere: in colonial papers, court records, published law codes such as *Hening's Statutes* for Virginia, private papers, published state papers, etc.

7. CALENDAR CHANGE.

In 1752, most western countries (Russia is the major exception) switched from the Julian Calendar to the Gregorian Calendar. Before 1752, each year began on March 25, and the year ran from March 25 to the following March 24. As a result, the first month of the year was March, the second April, the ninth November, and so on. Keep this in mind when you come across a reference to the 'seventh month of 1652.' That would be September, 1652.

Moreover, between January 1st and March 25th, dates were often written with both the present and the coming year, in this way: February 23rd 1712/13. Don't let this confuse you; it merely means 1712, almost 1713.

After 1752, the year of the calendar change, each year begins with January 1st, and the numbering of the months (as first month, sixth months, and so on) is the same as today.

8. COUNTY NAMES CHANGED.

Counties give birth to new counties as people give birth to people. Virginia, for example, had eight counties (or shires) in 1634. Naturally, these early counties were large. As the colony's government became more organized, more counties were created out of these eight. Partly this was done so every citizen could be within one day's ride of the county seat; in this way everyone could conduct business, petition the legislature, learn of official notices, etc. From only one of these early Virginia counties—Northumberland—116 counties were created. To make it even more confusing, some Virginia counties are now in West Virginia, some are in Kentucky, and some are extinct.

County records were kept at the county seat. Usually, they were housed in the courthouse or the clerk's office, or in a building close to one of those. When a new county was formed out of an existing one, what became of the records? Normally, they remained in the parent county; the new county's records would then begin from the date of its creation. Occasionally, some of the records were transferred to the new county, but not very often.

Most state archives have information about the development of the counties in their state. In Virginia, for example, that information is found in the booklet called *A Hornbook of Virginia History* (Richmond, Va.: Division of History of the Virginia Department of Conservation and Development, 1949).

Let's look at an example. Perhaps you learned that an ancestor owned some land near Stuart, Virginia, in what is now Patrick County. You think the land was in the family for several generations, and you want to find the records proving it. Patrick County was formed in 1791, so until you reach that date you can look in Patrick's records. Before 1791 though, you would have to look in the records of Patrick's parent county back to the date of its creation, then to its parent county, and so on. Here is a list of the counties Stuart, Virginia, would have been in had it existed in 1634 (the date in parenthesis is when that county was created):

Patrick (1791)—Henry (1777)—Pittsylvanie (1767)—Halifax

(1752)—Lunenburg (1746)—Brunswick (1732)—Prince George (1703)—Charles City County (1634).

As you can see, you might have to examine records in eight different counties. This is why it is helpful to go to the state archives and state library, located in that state's capital city in most cases. Copies of virtually all major county records are on microfilm in that one location. You would not have to travel to a number of different county seats to examine the records at each one of them.

Although every state archives will be able to tell you the derivation of its counties, a book that applies to the entire country, so would save you some letter-writing, is Kay Kirkham's *The Counties of the U.S., Their Derivation and Census Schedules* (Salt Lake City, Utah: Kay Publishing Co., 1961).

Once you find out the genealogy of the counties you're interested in, make up a chart for each one of them, showing when they were created, and what their parent and grandparent counties were, with their dates of creation. Also record on these charts any changes in state name or in state lines affecting that area. This will be a kind of road map to help you find your way in the jungle of county names.

9. PERIODS OF NO REQUIRED BIRTH CERTIFICATES.

Of course, the further back in time you trace, the harder it will be to find birth records. But even in modern times, gaps exist in birth records. Virginia, for instance, required no birth certificates between 1896 and 1912. For such gaps, other records such as driver's licenses, passports, and marriage records, along with recollections of living relatives can help you fill in the blanks.

10. DESTROYED RECORDS.

When you come to a place in your research where you absolutely have to have a certain record, and you find out it was destroyed when the county clerk's office burned in 1897, it can be a very frustrating experience.

I mentioned earlier that I researched a man who I believed was unjustly accused of falsification of records, among other wrongs. To prove my case I needed the Richmond, Virginia, court records for the period 1808-1815. I asked for them, and was told they had burned, along with many other records, when much of Richmond burned in 1865. I guarantee you that produced frustration! In this case, after an extensive search, I found what I needed to know (that he was innocent) in a newspaper account of the trial.

You may run into this problem of destroyed records at some point. Records were destroyed in one of three main ways: *by fires*—usually by the building burning in which the records were stored (most often this was the clerk's office); *by ravages of time*—records have been eaten by mice, bookworms, silverfish, etc., they have been damaged by mildew, water, heat and cold, or by the acid in the old ink gradually eating through the paper, and so on; *by wars*—soldiers moving through an area have little respect for official records. Often they will burn the clerk's office, or warm their hands in winter over fires built of burning papers, or they take home souvenirs. I saw a page from a will book that had been taken by a Connecticut soldier during the Civil War from Warwick County, Virginia's Court House; it

had a muddy boot print on it, and was partly burned. The soldier's descendants later kindly returned the item to the Virginia State Archives. Damage to American records by wars has been caused mostly by the Colonial Wars, Revolutionary War, War of 1812, the Indian Wars, and the Civil War.

How can you overcome the problem of destroyed or missing records? Here are some suggestions:

a. *Try alternative records.* If the will book was destroyed, try the deed book or court records. If the family Bible burned in an uncle's house fire, see if the State or county has birth, marriage, and death records; examine military and other records as well. For the different possible sources, see chapter two of this book.

b. If the records were destroyed since about 1930, *see if copies (microfilm or photostat) exist* in the state archives. Check the WPA Historical Records Survey of that state's records to see what existed and where it was located during the 1930's (Ask about these WPA Surveys at the state library or archives).

c. *Check the parent county's records.*

d. *Examine the records of neighboring counties.* The man you're seeking might have moved to another county; he might have owned land in more than one county, so would appear in a deed book. Also, any county in which he owned land received a copy of his will.

e. *Some of the missing records may have been reconstructed.* This is especially the case with some colonial records. For example, Virginia has had some English records pertaining to the Virginia colony microfilmed or otherwise copied, and copies of these records placed in the Virginia State Archives. Other states may have done the same for records from various time periods. Ask about this possibility at the state library or archives.

f. *Search diligently.* One genealogist, while rummaging through some old records at a county courthouse in Virginia, found a great number of what she described as 'loose papers.' These were miscellaneous papers filed with court cases, some marriage records, and lots of other things that proved to be a gold mine of genealogical information. So, if you really get stuck, go to the county courthouse and ask if they have any records you could rummage through.

Many times the state library or archives will have miscellaneous records from a county that are out of the ordinary, and you might not even realize they exist. Search through the card catalog at the library and the archives, and ask the archivists or librarians for any scrap of information. You might find something valuable.

g. There might have been more than one courthouse or clerk's office, etc., in that county. *Maybe only the records in one location were destroyed.*

h. *Check newspapers for the period.* They might tell you what records, if any, were saved, and where they were moved. Also, your ancestor might be mentioned in them. This can be time-consuming, because most newspapers are not indexed. But if it is the only possibility, it is worth the effort.

i. If local court records were destroyed, try district courts' or higher courts of appeals' records. These are often indexed.

j. Look in the *Who's Who* type books. If your ancestor is not listed in such a book, perhaps one of his or her relatives is mentioned, and that would help you.

k. Ask the people at the records center where you're working; they can be most helpful.

11. DISTANCE FROM THE RECORDS.

If you live too far from where the records you need are kept, you have several alternatives. One is to buy the reels of microfilm you need from the appropriate archives or records depository. If you buy more than a few microfilm reels, it can be expensive; the price of one reel from the National Archives is about $12 at this writing. Still, ten or even twenty reels of microfilm might be less expensive than a trip from California to Virginia or to Connecticut. Ask the appropriate archives for its microfilm listing and prices.

If you have relatives living in the state or not far from the state where the records are located, consider asking them if they would do some of the research for you. Offer to pay their expenses, and to send them a copy of all the family history you put together.

You might also write the chairman of the history department of a college or university near where the records are located. Ask him to send you the names of any graduate student (or, if none is available, undergraduate history majors) who would be willing to examine some records for you for a fee.

Also, check genealogical periodicals. Usually they have quite a few advertisements by people willing to search records in specified areas for a fee (these are records searchers, not professional genealogists). Write a few of these. If you decide to use one of them, be sure the two of you have clearly agreed in advance on fees, how often reports are to be made, and who can use the information found.

Finally, ask the appropriate state archives to recommend a professional genealogist to you. Usually, the archives will send you a list of five or ten people known by them to be reputable, but they will not recommend any one particular genealogist. Bear in mind that professional genealogists are expensive; however, if you can afford one, fine. If you do hire a professional, check out his or her credentials with the Board for Certification of Genealogists, 1307 New Hampshire Ave., N.W., Washington, D.C. 20036. Again, be certain you have a clear understanding about fees and other arrangements in advance.

You can always design a vacation trip around visits to locations of records you want to examine. You should always write ahead to the library, archives, or court house, to make sure the records you want to examine are on deposit there. Do go to the state library or state archives first, since they generally have nearly all official state and county records, and often quite a few private records as well.

12. COMPLETE ROADBLOCK.

If you have traced back as far as you can and have explored every avenue you can think of, but are still stuck, what can you do? The possibility exists that you may never find records on your missing person, but you will in most cases, if you stick to the search.

You may be dealing with a relative who, for one reason or another, decided to move to an unexpected location. Here is where your knowledge of American history will help. What were the adventurous people of those years doing? Were they going to California to mine gold? Were they in the cavalry in Montana? Did they take up bounty land after the Revolutionary War? Did they just decide one day to load their belongings in a covered wagon and head west? If you have ever read Laura Ingalls Wilder's *Little House on the Prairie* series, you were probably amazed (as I was) at how many times they moved, and how great was the distance they moved by covered wagon from Wisconsin to Indian Territory, to Minnesota, to the Dakotas, back to Missouri, etc.

You might have to search through many sources to find your missing ancestors, but you should eventually locate a good many of them. Advertise your need in one of the genealogical periodicals. In the meantime, work on your other lines where you do have available sources.

The point is that much of the fun of digging into your roots is the detective-like techniques you often have to use. I know from experience the delight and frustration of the search, and the deep satisfaction that comes from solving what seemed to be an impossible problem.

Of course, some problems will never be solved. This is especially so if you are dealing with ancestors whose traditions were oral, not written. If your ancestors are Black, or American Indian, etc., you will rapidly run head-on into this problem. Part of the value of Alex Haley's book *Roots* is the survival and relative accuracy of the oral tradition passed down from his African ancestor, Kunta Kinte. But even Haley could only trace where the oral tradition led him. He could find out nothing about most of his lines. If your ancestors were Black slaves, you will have great difficulties tracing them very far. But persevere; Alex Haley did, and the rewards were great. If you are stumped at every point, be proud that *Roots* in a sense is the family tree of every Black American.

Chapter Five
Foreign Research

Anytime you have to do ancestral research outside the United States, you will run into problems and expenses, both of which may be serious. If you still want to try it, here are a number of ways you can go about genealogical research in foreign countries:

1. *Visit there yourself,* and do research in appropriate records locations. This can be complex and expensive, especially if you have to do research in a foreign language. I have done a good bit of digging in sources in German, and I know from experience that unless you are familiar with not only the language, but also the handwriting, you will have serious problems.

2. *Hire a genealogical researcher from that country.* This can be filled with unforeseen pitfalls and expenses.

3. *Try to contact* relatives, friends, or pen pals who live in that country and ask them to help you. Offer in exchange to help them look up relatives they may have in the United States.

4. *Write the Mormons* (The Genealogical Society, 50 East North Temple St., Salt Lake City, Utah 84150). They have some foreign records on microfilm, and in papers and book form. Besides the usual European countries, they have records concerning the Pacific, south Asia, Africa, and the Middle East.

5. *Consult genealogical books in English* that pertain to the country or area you are researching. If you cannot find such

books in your local or state library, or the Library of Congress, look through the pages of genealogical periodicals; frequently, they have advertisements for books dealing with immigrants from specific foreign locations, etc. If you read the language of the country you're interested in, you may be able to find some foreign-language books in American libraries to help you.

6. *Your foreign family tree may have been done already.* If one of your ancestral families was prominent, or from nobility or royalty, you might find that research has already been done on that family. One of my lines, the Leftwich family, had been traced back to the 13th century. In any case, check local or state libraries, the Mormons, and the Library of Congress for the possibility that the work has already been done for you. It could save you an enormous amount of time and money.

For most of us, though, foreign research will be difficult, since most of us came from the 'common people.' For those, after a certain point around the 12th to 14th centuries, you will run into a blind alley. From those years on back nearly to the Roman Empire, people went by their first name, and if they had another name, it was often a term that denoted where they lived, what they did as a trade, or perhaps what they were like.* You might run into Eric the Red, John the Fat, Charles the Simple, Bodo the Beekeeper, Gandulf the Tinker, Harold Bluetooth, Johann of (von) Rothwesten, Attila the Hun, and so on. Unless continuous records have survived wars, flood, fires, insects, mildew, rats, and careless humans, you usually cannot trace your family tree any further once you reach that point. The one sure thing you can say from then on back is that you are related to Noah, and ultimately, to Adam and Eve. Anything else is speculation.

Let's say you have traced your family tree back to an ancestor who first came to America. What do you do then? First, be certain you have the correct spelling of the immigrant's original

---

*A fascinating book on the origins of family names is W. O. Hassall's *History Through Surnames* (Oxford: Pergamon Press, 1967). You might find other books on the history of surnames in your library.

name. If he or she came within the last century, the immigration and naturalization records should be helpful; often they will show place of birth. However, if he came before the Civil War and you're forced to use the passenger lists, you will find that all the records usually show under your man's name is the name of the port his ship left from, but not his home town.

Still, that need not be a dead end. The first step is to write the Embassy of that country in Washington, D.C. Simply address your letter to: The . . . (French, British, German, etc.) Embassy, Washington, D.C. Besides asking them for general information, ask them the address of their tourist office located in this country (tourist offices often have a pamphlet that discusses doing genealogical research in that country).

Here is a sampling of such booklets that you can write for from some foreign countries:

(Britain) *Tracing Your Ancestors*, free, from the British Tourist Authority, 680 Fifth Ave., New York, N.Y. 10019.

(Denmark) The Danish government has no specific finding aid. However, it recommends that you write the town tourist office if you know the town your ancestor came from. You might also contact the Genealogical Institute, Norre Volgade 80, 1358 Copenhagen K. They charge a fee to do research.

(Ireland) The Irish Tourist Board, 590 Fifth Ave., New York, N.Y. 10036, publishes a pamphlet of helps for ancestor hunters of Irish descent.

(Italy) The Italian Government Travel Office, 630 Fifth Ave., New York, N.Y. 10020, is not allowed to recommend individual genealogists. If you know the town or city where your ancestor came from, you might write the records office (ufficio anagrafo) in the town hall (municipio) of that town or city.

(Norway) *How To Trace Your Ancestors In Norway*, available free from the Norwegian National Tourist Office, 75 Rockefeller Plaza, New York, N.Y. 10019.

(Poland) Poland has no official publication. The Polish National Tourist Office, 500 Fifth Ave., New York, N.Y. 10036, recommends you write the following genealogical society that will do genealogical research for a fee: Naczelna Dyrekcja Archiwow Panstwowych, 10 Miodowa St., Warsaw, Poland.

(Switzerland) Write to the Swiss National Tourist Office, The Swiss Center, 608 Fifth Ave., New York, N.Y. 10020, for a list of Swiss genealogists who can help you.

Some books that may help you are these: Greenwood's *The Researcher's Guide to American Genealogy* has an excellent section in chapter 24 on Canadian research. Rubincam's *Genealogical Research: Methods and Sources* has a good section dealing with foreign research, including these subjects: feudal genealogy; royal and noble genealogy; England and Wales; Scotland; Ireland; Germany; Netherlands; France; Switzerland; Scandinavia. See also L. G. Pine's *American Origins: A Handbook of Genealogical Sources Throughout Europe* (1960).

Kaminkow's *Genealogies in the Library of Congress: A Bibliography* lists 'not only American and English works but also holdings of Canadian, Irish, Welsh, Scottish, Australian, Latin American, Polish, German, Dutch, Scandinavian, French, Spanish, Italian, Portuguese, and Asian sources.' The *Harvard Guide To American History* has information concerning foreign archives. So does Filby's *American and British Genealogy and Heraldry*. Look at biographical sources for foreign individuals as well. Some of these are: *The Dictionary of National Biography* (for Great Britain), *The International Who's Who*, and a number of others.

In addition, you should write the New York Public Library, American History and Genealogy Division, Fifth Ave. & 42nd St., New York, N.Y. 10018, and the National Genealogical Society, 1921 Sunderland Pl., N.W., Washington, D.C. 20036. Also see my list of books pertaining to foreign genealogy in the back of this book.

Finally, check the pages of genealogical periodicals. Often, I have seen books concerning immigrants and their origins advertised in these periodicals.

You may want to read a history of the countries from which your ancestors came. Any public library or university library can recommend appropriate history books. A good one for

Great Britain is Hall, Albion, and Pope, *A History of England and the Empire-Commonwealth* (Waltham, Mass.: Xerox College Publishing, 1971). For general world history, a good two-volume work is Wallbank and Taylor's *Civilization Past and Present* (Chicago, Ill.: Scott, Foresman & Co., 1961).

Read the article on the country or area you want to learn about in either *Encyclopaedia Britannica* or *World Book Encyclopedia*, for background information.

* * * * *

ANOTHER KIND OF FAMILY.

In the pages of this book, you have learned about tracing your connections to your ancestors and other family members. As you find more and more of them, you will experience the thrill of discovering that you are part of a much larger human family than you realized.

But did you know that you can belong to yet another kind of family? Whatever your age, whatever your background, whatever your race, God loves you very much, and He wants you to become one of His spiritual family. God is a king; by becoming His spiritual son or daughter, you become the child of a king. Your new Father will meet your deepest needs, whether they are spiritual, physical, or material.

How do you become a child of God? In many ways, it's like your physical life: you had to be born physically, and learn how to walk, talk, and live on earth; to become God's spiritual child, you have to be born spiritually, so you can begin to enjoy a new relationship with God, the Father. Jesus said to one man that he had to be born a second time. This is what he meant.

How do you go about being reborn? You need to realize that—unless you have already done what I am about to say—your whole life has been under your own control. God has not been in the driver's seat, you have. God asks that you recognize and confess that fact and the wrongs it has led to, and then that you ask His forgiveness, stop doing the old deeds, and turn control of your life over to Him.

If you do so, He cleanses you of all selfishness, wrongs, and sins. He can do this because, although we all deserve to be punished by God for our selfishness, He has already punished someone else for us (us includes *you*). He chose to allow His son Jesus to be beaten, pierced, and to shed His blood for us. It is as though you had been found guilty of murder, but someone else volunteered to go to the electric chair for you. 'For God so loved the world (including *you*) that He gave his only begotten Son, that whoever believes in Him will not perish, but have everlasting life.' (John 3:16). If you turn, and trust in Jesus and follow Him, God promises you complete forgiveness of everything you have ever done or been. If you do this, you will be reborn, you will become a child of God. You will enter a new, joyful relationship with God, one in which He pours out His love on you, He accepts you, He meets all that has been needed in your life.

If these words cause a response in you, if you have been searching for certainty deep inside yourself, then take the step Jesus is asking you to take: turn from controlling your own life, and turn your life over to Jesus. That is becoming a Christian; that is joining God's spiritual family, with its countless numbers of brothers and sisters.

If you have done this, tell someone else of your decision. Begin to read the Bible, especially Matthew, Mark, Luke, and John to learn about Jesus. Read the Psalms for encouragement and an example of an honest relationship with God. (I recommend a good modern translation like the *New International Version*, or an excellent paraphrase like the *Living Bible*). Find a group of Christians who are trying to practice Jesus' commandments, and share your needs and victories with them.

Here are some books that should help you further: Derek Prince, *The Foundation Series* (7 pamphlets; order from Derek Prince, P.O. Box 306, Ft. Lauderdale, Fla. 33302); Derek and Lydia Prince, *Appointment in Jerusalem* (Chosen Books); Francis J. Roberts, *Come Away My Beloved* (The King's Press, P.O. Box 763, Palos Verdes Estates, Calif. 90274); Francis A.

Schaeffer, *The Church At The End Of The Twentieth Century* (Inter-Varsity Press); John R. W. Stott, *Becoming a Christian*, and *Basic Christianity* (Inter-Varsity Press); Corrie Ten Boom, *The Hiding Place* (Chosen Books); A. W. Tozer, *The Pursuit of God* (Christian Publications, Inc., Harrisburg, Pa.); and Walter Trobisch, *Martin Luther's Quiet Time* (Inter-Varsity Press booklet).

Chapter Six
Useful Addresses

Here are some addresses of libraries, archives, and historical societies that I believe you will find useful. They are arranged alphabetically by state, and, within each state, alphabetically by name of the city where they are located.

ALABAMA

Draughon Library
Auburn University
Auburn, Alabama 36830

Southern Historical Collection
Birmingham Public and Jefferson
  County Free Library
2020 7th Ave., N
Birmingham, Alabama 35203

Mobile Public Library
701 Government Street
Mobile, Alabama 36602

Alabama Dept. of Archives and
  History
War Memorial Bldg.
624 Washington Ave.
Montgomery, Alabama 36104

Gorgas Library
University of Alabama

University, Alabama 35486

ALASKA

Adjutant General
National Guard
Anchorage, Alaska 99501

Archives and Manuscripts
Rasmuson Library
University of Alaska
Fairbanks, Alaska 99701

Alaska Historical Library
Alaska Division of State Libraries
State Office Bldg.
Juneau, Alaska 99801

Archives and Records Management
450 Whittier St.
Juneau, Alaska 99801

Special Collections
Sheldon Jackson College Library
Sitka, Alaska 99835

ARIZONA

Dept. of Library & Archives
Capitol Building, Third Floor
Phoenix, Arizona 85007

Arizona Historical Foundation
Hayden Library
Arizona State University
Tempe, Arizona 85281

Arizona Historical Society
949 East Second St.
Tucson, Arizona 85719

Tucson Public Library
200 South 6th
Tucson, Arizona 85701

University of Arizona Library
Tucson, Arizona 85721

ARKANSAS

University of Arkansas Library
Fayetteville Campus
Fayetteville, Arkansas 72701

Arkansas Collection
Ft. Smith Public Library
61 South 8th St.
Ft. Smith, Arkansas 72901

Arkansas History Commission Library
Old State House, West Wing
300 West Markham St.
Little Rock, Arkansas 72201

Department of State Lands
State Capitol
Little Rock, Arkansas 72201

University of Arkansas at Little Rock
  Library
University Ave. at 33rd St.
Little Rock, Arkansas 72204

CALIFORNIA

Bancroft Library
University of California
Berkeley, California 94720

Los Angeles County Museum of Natural
  History
900 Exposition Blvd.
Los Angeles, California 90007

Los Angeles Public Library
630 West 5th St.
Los Angeles, California 90017

Los Angeles Temple Genealogical Library

10741 Santa Monica Blvd.
Los Angeles, California 90025

California State Library
Library-Courts Bldg.
Sacramento, California 95809

California State Archives and Central Records
Depository
Office of the Secretary of State
1020 O St.
Sacramento, California 95814

Sutro Library
2130 Fulton St.
San Francisco, California 94117

Special Collections
Stanford University Library
Stanford, California 94305

COLORADO

Western Historical Collection
Norlin Library
University of Colorado
Boulder, Colorado 80302

Tutt Library
Colorado College
Colorado Springs, Colorado 80903

Colorado State Library
Department of Education
1362 Lincoln St.
Denver, Colorado 80203

Division of State Archives and Public
Records
1530 Sherman St.
Denver, Colorado 80203

State Historical Society of Colorado
Documentary Resources Dept.

200 14th Ave.
Denver, Colorado 80203

Western History Dept.
Denver Public Library
1357 Broadway
Denver, Colorado 80203

CONNECTICUT

Connecticut Historical Society
1 Elizabeth St.
Hartford, Conn. 06105

Connecticut State Library
231 Capitol Ave.
Hartford, Conn. 06115

Dept. of Special Collections
Cross Library
University of Connecticut
Storrs, Conn. 06268

New Haven Colony Historical Society
114 Whitney Ave.
New Haven, Conn. 06510

Yale University Library
120 High St.
New Haven, Conn. 06520

DELAWARE

Delaware Public Archives Commission
Hall of Records
Dover, Delaware 19901

Morris Library
University of Delaware
Newark, Delaware 19711

Eleutherian Mills Historical Library
Greenville
Wilmington, Delaware 19807

Historical Society of Delaware
505 Market St.
Wilmington, Delaware 19801

Genealogical Society of Pennsylvania
1300 Locust St.
Philadelphia, Pennsylvania 19107

DISTRICT OF COLUMBIA

Central Reference Division (NNC)
National Archives (GSA)
Washington, D.C. 20408

Columbia Historical Society
1307 New Hampshire Ave., NW
Washington, D.C. 20036

Dept. of Public Health
Vital Records Division
300 Indiana Ave., NW
Washington, D.C. 20001

Genealogy Division
Library of Congress
Washington, D.C. 20540

Library
National Society, Daughters of the
  American Revolution
1776 D St., NW
Washington, D.C. 20006

National Genealogical Society
1921 Sunderland Ave., NW
Washington, D.C. 20036

Recorder of Deeds
6th and D Streets, NW
Washington, D.C. 20004

Register of Wills
5th and E Streets, NW
Washington, D.C. 20001

FLORIDA

Polk County Historical Commission
511 Court House
Bartow, Florida 33830

Yonge Library of Florida History
University of Florida Library
Gainesville, Florida 32611

Orlando Public Library
10 North Rosalind
Orlando, Florida 32801

Bureau of Archives and Records
  Management
401 East Gaines St.
Tallahassee, Florida 32304

State Land Office
Elliot Building
Tallahassee, Florida 32304

Tampa-Hillsborough County Public
  Library
900 North Ashley St.
Tampa, Florida 33602

GEORGIA

Ilah Dunlap Little Memorial Library
University of Georgia
Athens, Georgia 30602

Atlanta Public Library
126 Carnegie Way, NW
Atlanta, Georgia 30303

Georgia Dept. of Archives and History
Central Research Divison
330 Capitol Ave., SE
Atlanta, Georgia 30334

Surveyor General Dept.
Archives and Records Bldg.

Atlanta, Georgia 30334

Woodruff Library
Emory University
Atlanta, Georgia 30333

Georgia State Library
301 State Judicial Bldg.
Capitol Hill Station
Atlanta, Georgia 30334

Washington Memorial Library
1180 Washington Ave.
Macon, Georgia 31201

Georgia Historical Society
501 Whitaker St.
Savannah, Georgia 31401

HAWAII

Hawaiian Historical Society
560 Kawaiahao St.
Honolulu, Hawaii 96813

Public Archives Library
Iolani Palace Grounds
Honolulu, Hawaii 96813

Sinclair Library
University of Hawaii
Honolulu, Hawaii 96822

State Library Branch
Hawaii State Library
478 South King St.
Honolulu, Hawaii 96813

Woolley Library
Church College of Hawaii
Laie, Hawaii 96762

IDAHO

Boise Branch Genealogical Library

325 West State St.
Boise, Idaho 83706

Idaho State Archives
325 West State St.
Boise, Idaho 83702

Idaho State Historical Society
Historical and Genealogical Library
610 N. Julia Davis Dr.
Boise, Idaho 83706

University of Idaho Library
Moscow, Idaho 83843

McKay Library
Ricks College
Rexburg, Idaho 83440

ILLINOIS

Newberry Library
60 West Walton St.
Chicago, Ill. 60610

Adjutant General
State Armory
Springfield, Ill. 62706

Illinois State Historical Society
  and Library
Old State Capitol
Springfield, Ill. 62706

State Archives
Archives Bldg.
Springfield, Ill. 62706

Champaign Library
University of Illinois at Urbana
Urbana, Ill. 61801

INDIANA

Lily Library

Indiana University
10th St. and Jordan Ave.
Bloomington, Indiana 47401

Public Library of Ft. Wayne and
   Allen County
900 Webster St.
Ft. Wayne, Ind. 46802

Archives Division, Indiana State Library
140 North Senate Ave.
Indianapolis, Ind. 46204

Indiana Historical Society and Library
140 North Senate Ave.
Indianapolis, Ind. 46204

Indiana State Library
140 North Senate Ave.
Indianapolis, Ind. 46204

IOWA

Davenport Museum
1717 West 12th St.
Davenport, Iowa 52804

Iowa State Dept. of History and Archives
Historical Bldg.
East 12th St. and Grand Ave.
Des Moines, Iowa 50319

State Historical Society of Iowa Library
Iowa and Gilbert Streets
Iowa City, Iowa 52240

University of Iowa Library
Iowa City, Iowa 52242

Marshalltown Community College Library
113 North First Ave.
Marshalltown, Iowa 50158

Sioux City Public Library
705 Sixth St.

Sioux City, Iowa 55105

KANSAS

Kansas Genealogical Society
700 Avenue G
Dodge City, Kansas 67801

Spencer Research Library
University of Kansas
Lawrence, Kansas 66045

Kansas State Archives
120 West 10th St.
Topeka, Kansas 66612

Kansas State Historical Society
120 West 10th St.
Topeka, Kansas 66612

Kansas State Library
3rd Floor, State House
Topeka, Kansas 66612

Topeka Genealogical Workshop
2110 North Topeka Ave.
Topeka, Kansas 66609

KENTUCKY

Kentucky Library and Museum
Western Kentucky University
Bowling Green, Kentucky 42101

Bureau of State Archives and Records
851 East Main St.
Frankfort, Kentucky 40601

Kentucky State Historical Society
Old State House
Frankfort, Kentucky 40601

King Library
University of Kentucky
Lexington, Kentucky 40506

LOUISIANA

Department of Archives and History
Louisiana State University Library
Baton Rouge, Louisiana 70803

Louisiana Historical Association
Box 44222-Capital Station
Baton Rouge, Louisiana 70804

Louisiana State Library
State Capitol Grounds
760 North Third St.
Baton Rouge, Louisiana 70821

State Archives and Records Commission
Capitol Station
Baton Rouge, Louisiana 70804

State Land Office
Capitol Station
Baton Rouge, Louisiana 70804

Louisiana Historical Society
Gallier Hall
545 St. Charles Ave.
New Orleans, Louisiana 70130

Louisiana State Museum
751 Chatres St.
New Orleans, Louisiana 70116

MAINE

Maine State Archives and Library
State Capitol
Augusta, Maine 04330

State Forestry Dept.
State Capitol
Augusta, Maine 04330

Bangor Public Library
145 Harlow St.
Bangor, Maine 04401

Fogler Library
University of Maine at Orono
Orono, Maine 04473

Maine Historical Society
485 Congress St.
Portland, Maine 04111

MARYLAND

Hall of Records
College Ave. and St. John's St.
Annapolis, Maryland 21404

Enoch Pratt Library
Peabody Library
17 East Mount Vernon Place
Baltimore, Maryland 21202

Maryland Historical Society
201 West Monument St.
Baltimore, Maryland 21201

Maryland Collection
McKeldin Library
University of Maryland
College Park, Maryland 20742

Blackwell Library
Salisbury State College
Camden and College Avenues
Salisbury, Maryland 21801

MASSACHUSETTS

Archives of the Commonwealth
Office of the Secretary
State House
Boston, Mass. 02133

Boston Public Library
Copley Square
666 Boylston St.
Boston, Mass. 02117

Massachusetts Historical Society
1154 Boylston St.
Boston, Mass. 02115

New England Historic Genealogical
   Society
101 Newbury St.
Boston, Mass. 02116

Bay State Historical League
8 Capon Rd.
Braintree, Mass. 02184

The Houghton Library
Harvard University Library
Cambridge, Mass. 02138

American Antiquarian Society
   Library
185 Salisbury St.
Worcester, Mass. 01609

MICHIGAN

Historical Society of Michigan
2117 Washtenaw Ave.
Ann Arbor, Mich. 48104

Michigan Historical Collection
Bentley Historical Library
University of Michigan
Ann Arbor, Mich. 48104

Burton Collection
Detroit Public Library
5201 Woodward Ave.
Detroit, Mich. 48202

Michigan State Archives
3405 North Logan St.
Lansing, Mich. 48918

Michigan State Library
735 East Michigan Ave.

Lansing, Mich. 48913

MINNESOTA

Memorial Library
Mankato State College
Mankato, Minn. 56001

Minneapolis Public Library
300 Nicollet Mall
Minneapolis, Minn. 55401

Wilson Library
University of Minnesota
Minneapolis, Minn. 55455

Centennial Hall Learning Resources
  Center
St. Cloud State College
St Cloud, Minn. 56301

Minnesota Historical Society
690 Cedar St.
St. Paul, Minn. 55101

Minnesota State Archives Commission
117 University Ave.
St. Paul, Minn. 55101

MISSISSIPPI

Evans Memorial Library
Aberdeen, Miss. 39730

Mississippi Dept. of Archives
  and History
War Memorial Bldg.
Capitol Green
Box 571
Jackson, Miss. 39205

Mississippi Historical Society
Archives and History Bldg.
Capitol Green
Jackson, Miss. 39205

Mitchell Memorial Library
Mississippi State University
State College, Miss. 39762

Museum Library
Old Court House
Vicksburg, Miss. 39180

MISSOURI

State Historical Society of
    Missouri
University Library Bldg.
Hitt and Lowry Streets
Columbia, Missouri 65201

Records Management and
    Archives Service
1011 Industrial Drive
Jefferson City, Missouri 65101

Kansas City Public Library
311 East 12th St.
Kansas City, Missouri 64106

History and Genealogy Room
St. Louis Public Library
1301 Olive St.
St. Louis, Missouri 63103

Missouri Historical Society Library
Jefferson Memorial Bldg.
Lindell and DeBaliviere Ave.
St. Louis, Missouri 63112

MONTANA

University Library
Montana State University
Bozeman, Montana 59715

Department of State Lands
State Capitol
Helena, Montana 59601

Montana Historical Society Library
225 North Roberts St.
Helena, Montana 59601

Montana State Library
930 East Lyndale Ave.
Helena, Montana 59601

University Library
University of Montana
Messoula, Montana 59801

NEBRASKA

Ryan Library
Kearney State College
Kearney, Nebraska 68847

Love Memorial Library
University of Nebraska
Lincoln, Nebraska 68508

Nebraska State Historical Society Library
1500 R. St.
Lincoln, Nebraska 68508

North Platte Public Library
120 West Fourth St.
North Platte, Nebraska 69101

Omaha Public Library
19th and Harney Streets
Omaha, Nebraska 68102

Peru State College Library
Peru, Nebraska 68421

NEVADA

Nevada State Library
Carson City, Nevada 89701

Nevada State Archives
Capitol Bldg.

Carson City, Nevada 89701

Dickinson Library
University of Nevada at Las Vegas
4505 Maryland Parkway
Las Vegas, Nevada 89154

Getchell Library
University of Nevada
Reno, Nevada 89507

Nevada State Historical Society
State Building
1650 North Virginia St.
Reno, Nevada 89504

NEW HAMPSHIRE

New Hampshire Historical Society
  Library
30 Park St.
Concord, New Hampshire 03301

New Hampshire State Library
20 Park St.
Concord, New Hampshire 03301

Records and Archives Center
71 South Fruit St.
Concord, New Hampshire 03301

Dover Public Library
73 Locust St.
Dover, New Hampshire 03820

NEW JERSEY

Savitz Learning Resource Center
Glassboro State College
Glassboro, New Jersey 08028

New Jersey Historical Society
230 Broadway
Newark, New Jersey 07104

Rutgers University Library

College Avenue
New Brunswick, New Jersey 08901

Dept. of Rare Books and Special
   Collections
Firestone Memorial Library
Princeton University
Princeton, New Jersey 08540

New Jersey State Library
185 West State St.
Trenton, New Jersey 08625

NEW MEXICO

Center for Learning and Information
   Resources
University of Albuquerque
St. Joseph Place
Albuquerque, New Mexico 87124

Zimmerman Library
University of New Mexico
Albuquerque, New Mexico 87106

Museum of New Mexico
Santa Fe, New Mexico 87501

New Mexico State Library
300 Don Gaspar
Santa Fe, New Mexico 87501

New Mexico State Records Center
   and Archives
404 Montezuma St.
Santa Fe, New Mexico 87501

NEW YORK

Division of Military and Naval Affairs
War Records
Bldg. 22, New York State Campus
Albany, New York 12226

New York State Library
Washington Ave.
Albany, New York 12225

Miscellaneous Records Division
162 Washington Ave.
Albany, New York 12225

Long Island Historical Society
128 Pierrepont St.
Brooklyn, New York 11201

Buffalo and Erie County Historical
    Society
25 Nottingham Court
Buffalo, New York 14216

New York State Historical
    Association
Lake Road
Cooperstown, New York 13326

Regional History and University
    Archives
Ohlin Library
Cornell University
Ithaca, New York 14850

New York Genealogical and Bio-
    graphical Society Library
122-126 East 58th St.
New York, New York 10022

New York Historical Society
    Library
170 Central Park West
New York, New York 10024

American History and Genealogy
    Division
New York Public Library
5th Avenue and 42nd St.
New York, New York 10018

NORTH CAROLINA

Pack Memorial Public Library
One S. Pack Square
Asheville, North Carolina 28801

Wilson Library
University of North Carolina
Chapel Hill, North Carolina 27514

Perkins Library
Duke University
Durham, North Carolina 27706

North Carolina State Library
Salisbury and Edenton Streets
P.O. Box 2889
Raleigh, North Carolina 27611

State Dept. of Archives and History
109 East Jones St.
Raleigh, North Carolina 27602

Rowan Public Library
201 West Fisher St.
Salisbury, North Carolina 28114

Smathers National Memorial Collections of
    Genealogical Records
Haywood County Public Library
Boyd Avenue
Waynesville, North Carolina 28786

NORTH DAKOTA

North Dakota State Historical Society
Liberty Memorial Bldg.
State Capitol Grounds
Bismarck, North Dakota 58501

State Land Dept.
Capitol Building
Bismarck, North Dakota 58501

North Dakota State Library Commission

83 High St.
Bismarck, North Dakota 58501

University Library
North Dakota State University
Fargo, North Dakota 58102

Libby Manuscript Collection
Fritz Library
University of North Dakota
Grand Forks, North Dakota 58201

Memorial Library
Minot State College
Minot, North Dakota 58701

OHIO

Alden Library
Ohio University
Athens, Ohio 45701

Cincinnati Historical Society
Eden Park
Cincinnati, Ohio 45202

Cleveland Public Library
325 Superior Ave.
Cleveland, Ohio 44114

Western Reserve Historical Society
  Library
10825 East Boulevard
Cleveland, Ohio 44106

Ohio State Historical Society
1813 N. High St.
Columbus, Ohio 43201

State Archivist
1234 E. Broad St.
Columbus, Ohio 43205

OKLAHOMA

Bizzell Memorial Library
University of Oklahoma
401 West Brooks St.
Norman, Oklahoma 73069

Oklahoma Historical Society
Historical Building
Oklahoma City, Oklahoma 73105

Oklahoma State Library and Division of Archives and Records
109 State Capitol
Oklahoma City, Oklahoma 73105

Genealogy Department
Tulsa City - County Library
400 Civic Center
Tulsa, Oklahoma 74103

Library
Thomas Gilcrease Institute
2501 West Newton, R. R. 6
Tulsa, Oklahoma 74127

OREGON

Memorial Library
University of Oregon
Eugene, Oregon 97403

Oregon Historical Society
1230 SW Park Ave.
Portland, Oregon 97205

Oregon State Archives
Oregon State Library
State Library Building
Salem, Oregon 97310

Willamette University Library

900 State Street
Salem, Oregon 97301

PENNSYLVANIA

Bureau of Land Records
South Office Bldg., Room 123
Commonwealth Ave.
Harrisburg, Pa. 15222

Genealogy and Local History Section
Pennsylvania State Library
Education Building
Harrisburg, Pa. 17108

Pennsylvania Historical and Museum
  Commission
William Penn Memorial Museum and
  Archives Building
Harrisburg, Pa. 17101

City History Society of Pennsylvania
  Library
4237 Sansom St.
Philadelphia, Pa. 19104

Free Public Library of Philadelphia
Logan Square
Philadelphia, Pa. 19103

Genealogical Society of Pennsylvania
1300 Locust St.
Philadelphia, Pa. 19107

Historical Society of Pennsylvania
1300 Locust St.
Philadelphia, Pa. 19107

University of Pennsylvania Library
3420 Walnut St.
Philadelphia, Pa. 19104

Carnegie Library of Pittsburgh
4400 Forbes Ave.

Pittsburgh, Pa. 15213

RHODE ISLAND

University of Rhode Island Library
Kingston, Rhode Island 02881

Newport Historical Society
82 Touro St.
Newport, Rhode Island 02840

Providence Public Library
229 Washington St.
Providence, Rhode Island 02903

Records Center
Veterans Memorial Building
83 Park Street
Providence, Rhode Island 02903

Rhode Island Historical Society
52 Powell St.
Providence, Rhode Island 02903

Rhode Island State Archives
314 State House
Providence, Rhode Island 02903

SOUTH CAROLINA

Charleston Library Society
164 King Street
Charleston, South Carolina 29401

South Carolina Historical Society
Fireproof Building
Charleston, South Carolina 29401

Free Library
404 King Street
Charleston, South Carolina 29407

South Carolina Dept. of Archives and
   History
1430 Senate Street

Columbia, South Carolina 29201

South Carolina Library
University of South Carolina
Columbia, South Carolina 29208

Greenville County Library
300 College Street
Greenville, South Carolina 29601

SOUTH DAKOTA

Public Lands Office
State House
Pierre, South Dakota 57501

South Dakota State Historical Society
Soldiers Memorial Building
Capitol Avenue
Pierre, South Dakota 57501

South Dakota State Library Commission
322 South Fort St.
Pierre, South Dakota 57501

Weeks Library
University of South Dakota
Vermillion, South Dakota 57069

TENNESSEE

Chattanooga Public Library
601 McCallie Avenue
Chattanooga, Tennessee 37403

Hoskins Library
University of Tennessee
Knoxville, Tennessee 37916

Knoxville - Knox Public Library
500 West Church Ave.
Knoxville, Tennessee 37902

Brister Library
Memphis State University

Southern and Patterson
Memphis, Tennessee 38152

Tennessee Historical Commission
State Library and Archives Bldg.
Nashville, Tennessee 37219

Tennessee State Library and
    Archives
403 7th Avenue North
Nashville, Tennessee 37219

TEXAS

Archives Division
Texas State Library
1201 Brazoo St.
Austin, Texas 78711

General Land Office
Texas State Library
1201 Brazoo St.
Austin, Texas 78711

Texas Historical Center
Lamar Library
University of Texas
Austin, Texas 78712

Dallas Public Library
1954 Commerce St.
Dallas, Texas 75201

Center for Genealogical Research
Clayton Library
5300 Caroline St.
Houston, Texas 77004

UTAH

Daughters of Utah Pioneers Library
Pioneer Memorial Museum
300 North Main St.
Salt Lake City, Utah 84102

The Genealogical Society
50 East North Temple
Salt Lake City, Utah 84150

Marriott Library
University of Utah
Salt Lake City, Utah 84112

State Archives
State Capitol Building
Salt Lake City, Utah 84114

Utah State Historical Society
603 East South Temple
Salt Lake City, Utah 84102

VERMONT

Genealogical Library
Bennington Museum
West Main Street
Bennington, Vermont 05201

Bailey Memorial Library
University of Vermont
Burlington, Vermont 05401

Public Records Division
State Administration Building
Montpelier, Vermont 05602

Vermont Historical Society
State Administration Building
Montpelier, Vermont 05602

VIRGINIA

Alderman Library
University of Virginia
Charlottesville, Virginia 22901

McCormick Library
Washington and Lee University
Lexington, Virginia 24450

Union Theological Seminary
3401 Brook Rd.
Richmond, Virginia 23227
  [for Presbyterian Church
    records]

Virginia Baptist Historical Society
University of Richmond, Virginia 23173

Virginia Historical Society
428 North Boulevard
Richmond, Virginia 23221

Virginia State Library and Archives
11th and Capitol Streets
Richmond, Virginia 23219

E.G. Swem Library
College of William and Mary
Williamsburg, Virginia 23185

WASHINGTON

Division of Archives and Records
  Management
12th and Washington Streets
Olympia, Washington 98501

Washington State Library
Olympia, Washington 98504

Seattle Public Library
1000 Fourth Ave.
Seattle, Washington 98104

Washington State University Library
Pullman, Washington 99163

University of Washington Library
Seattle, Washington 98105

Washington State Historical Society
315 North Stadium Way
Tacoma, Washington 99163

WEST VIRGINIA

Dept. of Archives and History
State Capitol Building
Room E-400
Charleston, West Virginia 25305

Land Division
State Capitol Building
Charleston, West Virginia 25305

Cabell County Public Library
900 5th Avenue
Huntington, West Virginia 25701

West Virginia Collection
West Virginia University Library
Morgantown, West Virginia 26506

WISCONSIN

McIntyre Library
University of Wisconsin
105 Garfield Avenue
Eau Claire, Wisconsin 54701

Division of Archives and Manuscripts
816 State St.
Madison, Wisconsin 53706

State Historical Society of Wisconsin
816 State St.
Madison, Wisconsin 53706

Milwaukee Public Library
814 West Wisconsin Ave.
Milwaukee, Wisconsin 53233

University of Wisconsin Library
2311 East Hartford Ave.
Milwaukee, Wisconsin 53201

WYOMING

Laramie County Library

2800 Central Avenue
Cheyenne, Wyoming 82001

Wyoming State Archives and
   Historical Department
State Office Building
Cheyenne, Wyoming 82001

Wyoming State Historical
   Society
State Office Building
Cheyenne, Wyoming 82001

University of Wyoming Library
13th and Ivinson Streets
Laramie, Wyoming 82071

PUERTO RICO

Puerto Rico General Archives
305 San Francisco Ave.
San Juan, Puerto Rico 00927

* * * * *

The following are the addresses of the various Federal Records Centers, branches of the National Archives:

BOSTON

Federal Archives and Records
   Center
380 Trapelo Rd.
Waltham, Mass. 02154
(Hours: 8-4:30 M - F. Serves Connecticut, Maine, Massachusetts, New Hampshire, Rhode Island, and Vermont)

NEW YORK

Federal Archives and Records Center
Building 22 - MOT Bayonne

Bayonne, N.J. 07002
(Hours: 8 - 5 M - F. Serves New Jersey,
New York, Puerto Rico and the Virgin
Islands)

PHILADELPHIA

Federal Archives and Records Center
5000 Wissahickon Ave.
Philadelphia, Pa. 19144
(Hours: 8 - 4:30 M - F. Serves Delaware,
Pennsylvania; for the loan of microfilm, also
serves the District of Columbia, Maryland,
Virginia, and West Virginia)

ATLANTA

Federal Archives and Records Center
1557 St. Joseph Ave.
East Point, Ga. 30344
(Hours: 8 - 4:30 M - F. Serves Alabama,
Georgia, Florida, Kentucky, Mississippi,
North Carolina, South Carolina, and Ten-
nessee)

CHICAGO

Federal Archives and Records Center
7358 S. Pulaski Rd.
Chicago, Ill. 60629
(Hours: 8 - 4:30 M - F. Serves Illinois,
Indiana, Michigan, Minnesota, Ohio,
and Wisconsin)

KANSAS CITY

Federal Archives and Records Center
2306 E. Bannister Rd.
Kansas City, Mo. 64131
(Hours: 8 - 4:30 M - F. Serves Iowa, Kansas,
Missouri, and Nebraska)

FORT WORTH

Federal Archives and Records Center
4900 Hemphill St. (building address)
P.O. Box 6216 (mailing address)
Fort Worth, Texas 76115
(Hours: 8 - 4:30 M- F. Serves Arkansas,
Louisiana, New Mexico, Oklahoma,
and Texas)

DENVER

Federal Archives and Records
  Center
Building 48, Denver Federal
  Center
Denver, Colorado 80225
(Hours: 7:30 - 4 M - F. Serves Col-
orado, Montana, North Dakota,
South Dakota, Utah, and Wyoming)

SAN FRANCISCO

Federal Archives and Records
  Center
1000 Commodore Dr.
San Bruno, Calif. 94066
(Hours: 7:45 - 4:15 M - F. Serves
California (except southern California),
Hawaii, Nevada (except Clark County),
and the Pacific Ocean area)

LOS ANGELES

Federal Archives and Records
  Center
24000 Avila Rd.
Laguna Niguel, Calif. 92677
(Hours: 8 - 4:30 M - F. Serves Arizona, the southern California counties
of Imperial, Inyo, Kern, Los Angeles,

Orange, Riverside, San Bernardino,
San Diego, San Luis Obispo, Santa
Barbara, and Ventura; and Clark
County, Nev.)

SEATTLE

Federal Archives and Records
  Center
6125 Sand Point Way NE
Seattle, Washington 98115
(Hours: 8 - 4:30 M - F. Serves Alaska,
Idaho, Oregon, and Washington)

Chapter Seven
Helpful Source Books

This chapter contains a list of books that may help you further. I have broken them down into different subjects for easier reference. I hope you find them useful.

1. BIOGRAPHIES, AUTOBIOGRAPHIES, DIARIES.

Allen, William. THE AMERICAN BIOGRAPHICAL DICTIONARY (Boston, Mass.: J. P. Jewett, 1857).

THE AMERICAN GENEALOGICAL-BIOGRAPHICAL INDEX TO AMERICAN GENEALOGICAL, BIOGRAPHICAL, AND LOCAL HISTORY MATERIALS (Middletown, Conn.: The Godfrey Memorial Library, 1952) (95 volumes, through the name Keyes, as of 1976).

APPLETON'S CYCLOPAEDIA OF AMERICAN BIOGRAPHY (N.Y.: D. Appleton, various editions, 1887-1900) (7 volumes).

BIOGRAPHY INDEX; A CUMULATIVE INDEX TO BIOGRAPHICAL MATERIAL IN BOOKS AND MAGAZINES, 1946- (N.Y.: H. W. Wilson Co., 1964).

THE CYCLOPAEDIA OF AMERICAN BIOGRAPHIES (Boston, Mass.: Cyclopaedia Publishing Co., 1903) (7 volumes).

Filby, P. William. AMERICAN AND BRITISH GENEALOGY AND HERALDRY (A SELECTED LIST OF BOOKS) (Chicago, Ill.: American Library Association, 1975)

INDEX TO AMERICAN GENEALOGIES AND TO GENE-
ALOGICAL MATERIAL CONTAINED IN ALL WORKS
AS TOWN HISTORIES, COUNTY HISTORIES, LOCAL
HISTORIES, HISTORICAL SOCIETY PUBLICATIONS,
BIOGRAPHIES, HISTORICAL PERIODICALS, AND
KINDRED WORKS (Baltimore, Md.: Genealogical Publish-
ing Co., 1967 reprint).

Kaminkow, Marion. GENEALOGIES IN THE LIBRARY
OF CONGRESS: A BIBLIOGRAPHY (Baltimore, Md.: Magna Carta Publishing Co., 1972) (2 volumes).

Kaplan, Louis, and others. A BIBLIOGRAPHY OF AMERI-
CAN AUTOBIOGRAPHIES (Madison, Wisc.: University of
Wisconsin Press, 1961).

Matthews, William. AMERICAN DIARIES IN MANU-
SCRIPT, 1580-1950: A DESCRIPTIVE BIBLIOGRAPHY
(Athens, Ga.: University of Georgia Press, 1974).

Matthews, William, and Pearce, Roy. AMERICAN DIARIES:
AN ANNOTATED BIBLIOGRAPHY OF AMERICAN
DIARIES WRITTEN PRIOR TO THE YEAR 1861 (Berkeley:
University of California Press, 1945).

2. BLACK GENEALOGY.

Blockson, Charles L. BLACK GENEALOGY (Englewood
Cliffs, N.J.: Prentice-Hall, Inc.).

3. BOOKSTORES.

Genealogical Book Company, 521-523 St. Paul Place, Baltimore, Md. 21202. Ask for their free brochure of books they
have for sale.

Goodspeed's Book Shop, Inc., 18 Beacon St., Boston, Mass.
02108. Send $1.50 (at this writing) for their CATALOG OF
FAMILY AND LOCAL HISTORY. It lists more than 2,660
individual family histories, and more than 2,000 local histories,
as well as other materials.

In the pages of the NEW YORK TIMES you will find classified
advertisements placed by bookstores which carry used books;

many of these stores will try to locate for you rare or out-of-print books. Ask them about this service.

Charles E. Tuttle, Co., Inc., Rutland, Vermont 05701. Write for their catalog (the cost at this writing is $2.00). Entitled GENE-ALOGY AND LOCAL HISTORY, it lists more than 3,000 genealogies, as well as 3,500 additional items.

4. BOUNTY LANDS.

Brumbaugh, Gaius M. REVOLUTIONARY WAR REC-ORDS (Baltimore, Md.: Genealogical Publishing Co., 1967 reprint).

Donaldson, Thomas. THE PUBLIC DOMAIN (Public Land Commission, Committee on Codification, Washington, D.C.: U.S. Government Printing Office, 1884).

Robbins, Roy M. OUR LANDED HERITAGE: THE PUB-LIC DOMAIN 1776-1936 (Lincoln, Neb.: University of Nebraska Press, 1962).

5. CENSUS RECORDS.

Franklin, Neil W. 'Availability of Federal Population Census Schedules in the States,' NATIONAL GENEALOGICAL SO-CIETY QUARTERLY, Vol. 50 (1962), pp. 19-25, 101-109, 126; Vol. 51 (1963), pp. 16, 165-167.

HEADS OF FAMILIES; FIRST CENSUS OF THE UNITED STATES - 1790 (Spartanburg, S.C.: The Reprint Co., 154 W. Cleveland Park Dr., Spartanburg, S.C. 29303).

Rider, Fremont, ed. AMERICAN GENEALOGICAL INDEX (Middletown, Conn.: Godfrey Memorial Library, 1942-52; new series begun 1952). Indexes the 1790 Census, has 43 volumes of records of Revolutionary War soldiers, and many family genealogies. At present, the new series has completed 89 volumes. Highly recommended.

U.S. Census Bureau. A CENTURY OF POPULATION GROWTH FROM THE FIRST CENSUS OF THE UNITED STATES TO THE TWELFTH, 1790-1900 (Baltimore, Md.: Genealogical Publishing Co., 1967 reprint).

6. CHURCH RECORDS.

Binsfield, Edmund L. 'Church Archives in the United States and Canada,' AMERICAN ARCHIVIST, July 1958, Vol. 21, No. 3, pp. 311-332.

Gaustad, Edwin S. HISTORICAL ATLAS OF RELIGION IN AMERICA (N.Y.: Harper & Row, 1962).

Kirkham, Kay. A SURVEY OF AMERICAN CHURCH RECORDS, FOR THE PERIOD BEFORE THE CIVIL WAR, EAST OF THE MISSISSIPPI RIVER (Salt Lake City, Utah: Deseret Book Co., 1959/60).

Manross, William W. THE FULHAM PAPERS IN THE LAMBETH PALACE LIBRARY (Oxford: The Clarendon Press, 1965). Good for the colonial period.

Mead, Frank S. HANDBOOK OF DENOMINATIONS IN THE UNITED STATES (Nashville, Tenn.: Abingdon Press, 1970).

Rodda, Dorothy, and Harvey, John. DIRECTORY OF CHURCH LIBRARIES (Philadelphia: Drexel Press, 1967).

7. CITY RECORDS.

Kirkham, Kay. A HANDY GUIDE TO RECORD-SEARCHING IN THE LARGER CITIES OF THE UNITED STATES: INCLUDING A GUIDE TO THEIR VITAL RECORDS AND SOME MAPS WITH STREET INDEXES WITH OTHER INFORMATION OF GENEALOGICAL VALUE (Logan, Utah: Everton Publishers, Inc., 1974).

8. COLONIAL RECORDS.

COLONIAL RECORDS OF VIRGINIA (Baltimore, Md.: Genealogical Publishing Co., 1964).

Cognets, Louis des, Jr. ENGLISH DUPLICATES OF LOST VIRGINIA RECORDS (Princeton, N.J.: Louis des Cognets, Jr., P.O. Box 163, 1958).

Meynen, Emil, ed. BIBLIOGRAPHY ON GERMAN SETTLEMENTS IN COLONIAL NORTH AMERICA

(Detroit, Mich.: Gale Research Co., 1966 reprint).

THE NATIONAL UNION CATALOG OF MANUSCRIPT COLLECTIONS (Some of these are published in Ann Arbor, Michigan by J. W. Edwards; some in Hamden, Conn., by Shoe String Press; others in Washington, D.C. by the Library of Congress).

Also, write specific state archives and state libraries, and ask about their holdings of colonial records.

9. COUNTY NAMES, WHEN COUNTIES WERE FORMED, ETC.

Kane, Joseph. THE AMERICAN COUNTIES (N.Y.: The Scarecrow Press, Inc., 1960). Has origins, dates of creation, organization, population, etc.

Kirkham, Kay. THE COUNTIES OF THE U.S., THEIR DERIVATION AND CENSUS SCHEDULES (Salt Lake City, Utah: Kay Publishing Co., 1961).

Peterson, Clarence S. CONSOLIDATED BIBLIOGRAPHY OF COUNTY HISTORIES IN FIFTY STATES IN 1961 (Baltimore, Md.: Geneaological Publishing Co., 1963 reprint).

10. DIRECTORIES.

Klein, Bernard, ed. GUIDE TO AMERICAN DIRECTORIES (N.Y.: B. Klein and Co., 1972).

11. ETHNIC SOCIETIES, ETHNIC PUBLICATION.

Michigan State University has published a directory of ethnic publications, as well as a directory of ethnic studies librarians. Write them at the Publications Office, Michigan State University, Grand Rapids, Michigan 49502.

Wynar, Lubomyr R. ENCYCLOPEDIC DIRECTORY OF ETHNIC NEWSPAPERS AND PERIODICALS IN THE UNITED STATES (Littleton, Colorado: Libraries Unlimited, 1972).

12. FOREIGN RESEARCH.

British Information Services, 845 Third Ave., New York, N.Y. 10022, publishes a catalog called RECORD PUBLICATIONS (ask for the latest edition). It contains some items useful for genealogical research, such as Scottish Deed Book Indexes, and other items.

THE BRITISH PUBLIC RECORD OFFICE (Richmond, Va.: Virginia State Library, 1960). This is a useful general guide. Besides a description of the Public Record Office it contains references to records of passengers on board ships bound for America, convicts transferred to Carolina and Virginia, and some Loyalist data.

BURKE'S GENEALOGICAL AND HERALDIC HISTORY OF THE PEERAGE BARONETAGE AND KNIGHTAGE (London: Burke's Peerage, Ltd., published every three or four years). Deals only with important families.

Falley, Margaret D. IRISH AND SCOTCH-IRISH ANCESTRAL RESEARCH (Margaret D. Falley, 999 Michigan Ave., Evanston, Ill., 1962).

Filby, P. William. AMERICAN AND BRITISH GENEALOGY AND HERALDY (A SELECTED LIST OF BOOKS) (Chicago, Ill.: American Library Association, 1975) (2nd Ed.).

Gardner, David E., and Smith, Frank. GENEALOGICAL RECORDS IN ENGLAND AND WALES (Salt Lake City, Utah: Bookcraft Publishers, 1956).

Grimble, Ian. SCOTTISH CLANS AN GENEALOGICAL RECORDS IN ENGLAND AND WALES (Salt Lake City, Utah: Bookcraft Publishers, 1956).

Grimble, Ian. SCOTTISH CLANS AND TARTANS (N.Y.: Tudor Publishing Co., 1973).

HARVARD GUIDE TO AMERICAN HISTORY (Cambridge, Mass.: The Belknap Press of Harvard University Press, 1974) (2 volumes). Has information concerning foreign archives on pages 100 through 105.

Kaminkow, Marion J., ed. GENEALOGIES IN THE LI-
BRARY OF CONGRESS, A BIBLIOGRAPHY (Baltimore,
Md.: Magna Carta Book Co., 1972 (2 volumes). Lists 'not only
American and English works but also holdings of Canadian,
Irish, Welsh, Scottish, Australian, Latin American, Polish, Ger-
man, Dutch, Scandinavian, French, Spanish, Italian, Portu-
guese, and Asian sources.'

MORMON RECORDS. Write The Genealogical Society, 50
East North Temple St., Salt Lake City, Utah 84150. Among
their records are sources from the Pacific area, South Asia, Africa, and the Middle East.

Phillimore, W.P.W. HOW TO WRITE THE HISTORY OF A
FAMILY (Detroit, Mich.: Gale Research Co., 1962 reprint).
Concerns English and Welsh genealogical research.

Pine, L. G. AMERICAN ORIGINS: A HANDBOOK OF
GENEALOGICAL SOURCES THROUGHOUT EUROPE
(1960).

PUBLISHER'S AND SEARCHER'S GUIDE (Published annually since 1971 by House of York, 1323 Wylie Way, San Jose,
Calif. 95130). Lists what the 70 companies they represent offer
for sale in the form of published genealogical books, etc.
Among their materials are foreign genealogies from Britain and
Europe, as well as family Bible records and wills for the same
area.

Rubincam, Milton, ed. GENEALOGICAL RESEARCH:
METHODS AND SOURCES (Washington, D. C.: The American Society of Genealogists, 1960). Has sections on feudal genealogy, royal and noble genealogy, England and Wales, Scotland, Ireland, Germany, Netherlands, France, Switzerland, and
Scandinavia.

Smith, Frank. A GENEALOGICAL GAZETEER OF EN-
GLAND (AN ALPHABETICAL DICTIONARY OF
PLACES WITH THEIR LOCATION, ECCLESIASTICAL
JURISDICTION, POPULATION, AND THE DATE OF
THE EARLIEST ENTRY IN THE REGISTER OF EVERY
ANCIENT PARISH IN ENGLAND) (Baltimore, Md.: Gene-

alogical Publishing Co., 1968).

Walne, Peter. ENGLISH WILLS (Richmond, Va.: Virginia State Library, 1964). Discusses probate records in England and Wales with a brief note on Scottish and Irish wills.

13. FRATERNAL ORDERS.

Ferguson, Charles W. FIFTY MILLION BROTHERS: A PANORAMA OF AMERICAN LODGES AND CLUBS (N.Y.: Farrar and Rhinehart, 1937).

14. GENEALOGICAL SOCIETIES.

Brown, Erma L.S. UNITED STATES GENEALOGICAL SO-CIETIES AND PUBLICATIONS (Salem, Oregon, 1974).

Meyer, Mark K., ed. DIRECTORY OF GENEALOGICAL SOCIETIES IN THE U.S.A. AND CANADA WITH AN AP-PENDED LIST OF INDEPENDENT GENEALOGICAL PERIODICALS (Published by M. K. Meyer, Rt. 10, Box 138-A, Pasadena, Md. 21122, 1976).

15. GENEALOGIES, PUBLISHED.

AMERICAN AND ENGLISH GENEALOGIES IN THE LI-BRARY OF CONGRESS (Baltimore, Md.: Genealogical Pub-lishing Co., 1967 reprint).

THE AMERICAN GENEALOGICAL-BIOGRAPHICAL INDEX TO AMERICAN GENEALOGICAL, BIOGRAPHI-CAL AND LOCAL HISTORY MATERIALS (Middletown, Conn.: The Godfrey Memorial Library, 1952). (95 volumes published by 1976, through the name Keyes).

THE AMERICAN GENEALOGIST, BEING A CATALOG OF FAMILY HISTORIES PUBLISHED IN AMERICA FROM 1771 TO DATE (Detroit, Mich: Gale Research Co., 1967 reprint of 5th edition of 1900).

BIBLIOGRAPHY OF AMERICAN GENEALOGY (Chica-go, Ill.: The Institute of American Genealogy, 1929).

Boddie, John. HISTORICAL SOUTHERN FAMILIES (Redwood City, Calif.: Pacific Coast Publishers, 1959) (13 volumes).

BURKE'S GENEALOGICAL AND HERALDIC HISTORY OF THE PEERAGE BARONETAGE AND KNIGHTAGE (London: Burke's Peerage, Ltd., published each three or four years).

A CATALOG OF GENEALOGICAL BOOKS IN PRINT (Springfield, Va.: Genealogical Books In Print, 6818 Lois Dr., Springfield, Va. 22150) (Lists over 5,000 titles). Cost is $4.00 at this writing.

Daughters of the American Revolution. CATALOG OF THE GENEALOGICAL AND HISTORICAL WORKS IN THE LIBRARY OF THE NATIONAL SOCIETY, DAUGHTERS OF THE AMERICAN REVOLUTION (Washington, D.C.: D.A.R., 1940).

Daughters of the American Revolution. D.A.R. LINEAGE BOOK (Washington, D.C.: D.A.R., various years, published in a number of volumes).

Genealogical Book Co., 521-523 St. Paul Place, Baltimore, Md. 21202, will send you a free brochure listing their books, if you request it.

GENEALOGY AND LOCAL HISTORY: AN ARCHIVAL AND BIBLIOGRAPHIC GUIDE (Evanston, Ill.: The Associates, 1959).

Goodspeed's Book Shop, Inc., 18 Beacon St., Boston, Mass. 02108, has a catalog of family and local history; it lists more than 2,660 individual family histories, and more than 2,000 local histories. Cost is $1.50 at this writing.

INDEX TO AMERICAN GENEALOGIES AND TO GENEALOGICAL MATERIAL CONTAINED IN ALL WORKS SUCH AS TOWN HISTORIES, COUNTY HISTORIES . . . [ETC.] (Albany, N.Y.: Joel Munsell's Sons, Publishers, 1900).

Kaminkow, Marion. GENEALOGIES IN THE LIBRARY OF CONGRESS: A BIBLIOGRAPHY (Baltimore, Md.: Magna Carta Publ. Co., 1972) (2 volumes). This contains probably the majority of genealogies which have been printed.

The Newberry Library, 60 West Walton St., Chicago, Ill. 60610, has published a 4 volume genealogical index, based on the books on genealogy in their library. Additions to this index were discontinued in 1918, but it might be helpful nevertheless. To see the particular books they have, you must go to the Newberry Library itself.

NEW ENGLAND HISTORICAL AND GENEALOGICAL REGISTER; CONSOLIDATED INDEX, VOLUMES 1-50 (Baltimore, Md.: Genealogical Publishing Co., 1972 reprint).

New York Public Library. DICTIONARY CATALOG OF THE LOCAL HISTORY AND GENEALOGY DIVISION, THE RESEARCH LIBRARIES OF THE NEW YORK PUBLIC LIBRARY (Boston, Mass.: G. K. Hall, 1974) (18 volumes). This book lists 295,000 cards representing 113,000 volumes.

PUBLISHER'S AND SEARCHER'S GUIDE (Published by House of York, 1323 Wylie Way, San Jose, Calif. 95130, appears annually since 1971). Lists material that 70 different companies have for sale. This is not an exhaustive catalog, but does have a great deal of useful material, including published genealogies.

Rider, Fremont, ed. AMERICAN GENEALOGICAL INDEX (Middletown, Conn.: Godfrey Memorial Library, 1959-52; new series begun in 1952) (89 volumes to date, completed through the name Daisy Jacobs).

Second-Hand Bookstores. Look in the classified section of major metropolitan newspapers such as the NEW YORK TIMES for advertisements by these types of bookstores. If they don't have the genealogical or other book you're looking for, they can often locate it for you.

Stewart, Robert A. INDEX TO PRINTED VIRGINIA GENEALOGIES (Richmond, Va.: Old Dominion Press, 1930). This book is an example of what is available for virtually all the states in the U.S.A.

Toedteberg, Emma, ed. CATALOGUE OF AMERICAN GENEALOGIES IN THE LIBRARY OF THE LONG ISLAND HISTORICAL SOCIETY (Baltimore, Md.: Genealogical Publishing Co., 1969 reprint).

Charles E. Tuttle Co., Inc., Rutland, Vermont 05701, has a catalog called GENEALOGY AND LOCAL HISTORY that 'lists over 3,000 genealogies and 3,500 additional items.' Price at this writing is $2.00.

Virkus, Frederick A., ed. THE ABRIDGED COMPENDIUM OF AMERICAN GENEALOGY (Chicago, Ill.: A. N. Marquis & Co., 1925-1943) (7 volumes).

Whittemore, Henry. GENEALOGICAL GUIDE TO THE EARLY SETTLERS OF AMERICA WITH A BRIEF HISTORY OF THOSE OF THE FIRST GENERATION (Baltimore, Md.: Genealogical Publishing Co., 1967).

16. HANDWRITING.

Kirkham, Kay. HOW TO READ THE HANDWRITING AND RECORDS OF EARLY AMERICA (Salt Lake City, Utah: Kay Publishing Co., 1961).

17. HERALDRY.

Scott-Giles, C. W. BOUTELL'S HERALDRY (London & N.Y.: Frederick Warne & Co., Ltd., 1958).

(In addition, most libraries have several books on heraldry; look in their card catalog.)

18. HISTORICAL SOCIETIES, LIBRARIES, MANUSCRIPT DEPOSITORIES, AND ARCHIVES.

DIRECTORY OF HISTORICAL SOCIETIES AND AGENCIES IN THE UNITED STATES AND CANADA (n.p.: American Association for State and Local History, 1959).

DIRECTORY OF STATE AND PROVINCIAL ARCHIVISTS (Nashville, Tenn.: Society of American Archivists, 1971).

Hamer, Philip M., ed. GUIDE TO ARCHIVES AND MANU-

SCRIPTS IN THE UNITED STATES (New Haven, Conn.: Yale University Press, 1961).

Historical Magazines. Almost every state has one of these. That state's State Library would know the name of it, and would have copies of its past and present issues.

McDonald, Donna, ed. DIRECTORY OF HISTORICAL SOCIETIES AND AGENCIES IN THE UNITED STATES AND CANADA (Nashville, Tenn.: American Association for State and Local History, appears annually).

NATIONAL UNION CATALOG OF MANUSCRIPT COLLECTIONS (Washington, D.C.: Library of Congress, 1959). This catalog lists over 27,000 manuscript collections on deposit in more than 800 locations.

19. HISTORY.

A GUIDE TO THE STUDY OF THE UNITED STATES OF AMERICA (Washington, D.C.: Library of Congress, 1960). This has an impressive list of books pertaining to every aspect of American history.

HARVARD GUIDE TO AMERICAN HISTORY (Cambridge, Mass.: The Belknap Press of Harvard University Press, 1974). This book is excellent; I recommend it highly.

MAKERS OF AMERICA (Chicago, Ill.: Encyclopaedia Britannica Educational Corp., 1971) (10 volumes). These include documents, letters, etc., and are a very good look at the wonderful variety of the ethnic melting pot that we call America.

Vol. I—THE FIRSTCOMERS (1536-1800)
Vol. II—BUILDERS OF A NEW NATION (1801-1848)
Vol. III—SEEKERS AFTER FREEDOM (1849-70)
Vol. IV—SEEKERS AFTER WEALTH (1871-90)
Vol. V—NATIVES AND ALIENS (1891-1903)
Vol. VI—THE NEW IMMIGRANTS (1904-13)
Vol. VII—HYPHENATED AMERICANS (1914-24)
Vol. VIII—CHILDREN OF THE MELTING POT (1924-38)
Vol. IX—REFUGEES AND VICTIMS (1939-54)

Vol. X—EMERGENT MINORITIES (1955-70)

Morison, Samuel Eliot. THE OXFORD HISTORY OF THE AMERICAN PEOPLE (N.Y.: Oxford University Press, 1965).

Sloane, Eric. DIARY OF AN EARLY AMERICAN BOY (NOAH BLAKE, 1805) (N.Y.: Ballentine Books, No. 24385). I warmly recommend everything Eric Sloane has written. He has books on barns, early American tools, and so on, all beautifully illustrated and very accurate and fascinating.

State Historical Booklets. Most states in the U.S. have published a small booklet about the history of their state, along with other details, such as how their counties were formed, and other facts. That kind of booklet for Virginia is called A HORNBOOK OF VIRGINIA HISTORY (Richmond, Va.: Division of History of the Virginia Department of Conservation and Development, 1949, edited by J. R. V. Daniel). Ask your state's archives or library about its historical booklet.

Wilder, Laura Ingalls. LITTLE HOUSE ON THE PRAIRIE (N.Y.: Harper & Row, various years). This book, along with Mrs. Wilder's seven other books about her family's travels west in a covered wagon, and what happened to them as they homesteaded in different places, can teach you more about life in the western U.S. in the late 19th century than any other source I know.

20. HOW-TO BOOKS.

Doane, Gilbert H. SEARCHING FOR YOUR ANCESTORS, THE HOW AND WHY OF GENEALOGY (Minneapolis, Minn.: University of Minnesota Press, 1960).

The Boy Scouts of America have published a Merit Badge handbook on Genealogy. Ask about this at stores that sell Boy Scout equipment and booklets.

Everton, George B., Sr., and Rasmuson, Gunnar. THE HANDY BOOK FOR GENEALOGISTS (Logan, Utah: The Everton Publishers, 1957).

Greenwood, Val D. THE RESEARCHER'S GUIDE TO

AMERICAN GENEALOGY (Baltimore, Md.: Genealogical Publishing Co., Inc., 1974).

Rubincam, Milton, ed. GENEALOGICAL RESEARCH: METHODS AND SOURCES (Washington, D.C.: The American Society of Genealogists, 1960).

21. HUGUENOTS.

Baird, Charles W. HISTORY OF THE HUGUENOT EMIGRATION TO AMERICA (Baltimore, Md.: Regional Publishing Co., 1966) (2 volumes). This is a history but it has the names of some Huguenots who came to America.

Brock, R. A., ed. DOCUMENTS CHIEFLY UNPUBLISHED, RELATING TO THE HUGUENOT EMIGRATION TO VIRGINIA AND THE SETTLEMENT AT MANAKIN TOWN—WITH AN APPENDIX OF GENEALOGIES (Richmond, Virginia: Virginia Historical Society, 1886).

22. IMMIGRANTS.

Banks, Charles E. TOPOGRAPHICAL DICTIONARY OF 2885 ENGLISH EMIGRANTS TO NEW ENGLAND 1620-1650 (Baltimore, Md.: Southern Book Co., 1957).

Bolton, Ethel. IMMIGRANTS TO NEW ENGLAND, 1700-1775 (Baltimore, Md.: Genealogical Publishing Co., 1966 reprint).

BRISTOL AND AMERICA; A RECORD OF THE FIRST SETTLERS IN THE COLONIES OF NORTH AMERICA, 1654-1685, INCLUDING THE NAMES WITH PLACES OF ORIGIN OF MORE THAN 10,000 SERVANTS TO FOREIGN PLANTATIONS WHO SAILED FROM . . . BRISTOL TO VIRGINIA, MARYLAND . . . [ETC.] (London: R. S. Glover, 1929).

Dickson, Robert J. ULSTER EMIGRATION TO COLONIAL AMERICA, 1718-1775 (London: Routledge and Kegan Paul, 1966).

Egle, William H. NAMES OF FOREIGNERS WHO TOOK

THE OATH OF ALLEGIANCE TO THE PROVINCE AND STATE OF PENNSYLVANIA, 1727-1775, WITH THE FOREIGN ARRIVALS, 1786-1808 (Baltimore, Md.: Genealogical Publishing Co., 1967 reprint).

Greer, George C. EARLY VIRGINIA IMMIGRANTS 1623-1666 (Baltimore, Md.: Genealogical Publishing Co., 1960).

Holmes, Frank R. DIRECTORY OF THE ANCESTRAL HEADS OF NEW ENGLAND FAMILIES 1620-1700 (Baltimore, Md.: Genealogical Publishing Co., 1964).

Hotten, John C., ed. THE ORIGINAL LISTS OF PERSONS OF QUALITY: EMIGRANTS; RELIGIOUS EXILES; APPRENTICES ... [ETC.] WHO WENT FROM GREAT BRITAIN TO THE AMERICAN PLANTATIONS 1600-1700. WITH THEIR AGES, THE LOCALITIES WHERE THEY FORMERLY LIVED IN THE MOTHER COUNTRY, THE NAMES OF THE SHIPS IN WHICH THEY EMBARKED ... [ETC.] (N.Y.: G. A. Baker & Co., 1931).

Kaminkow, Jack, and Kaminkow, Marion. A LIST OF EMIGRANTS FROM ENGLAND TO AMERICA, 1718-1759 (Baltimore, Md.: Magna Carta Book Co., 1964).

Kaminkow, Marion. GENEALOGIES IN THE LIBRARY OF CONGRESS: A BIBLIOGRAPHY (Baltimore, Md.: Magna Carta Publishing Co., 1972) (2 volumes).

Lancour, Harold. A BIBLIOGRAPHY OF SHIP PASSENGER LISTS 1538-1825 BEING A GUIDE TO PUBLISHED LISTS OF EARLY IMMIGRANTS TO NORTH AMERICA (N.Y.: The New York Public Library, 1963).

Lester, Annie L., and Hiden, Martha W., eds. ADVENTURERS OF PURSE AND PERSON: VIRGINIA 1607-1625 (Princeton, N.J.: Princeton University Press, 1956).

Lists of Germans from the Palatinate Who Came to England in 1709,' THE NEW YORK GENEALOGICAL AND BIOGRAPHICAL RECORD, XL (1909), pp. 49-54, 93-100, 160-167, 241-248; XLI (1910), pp. 10-19.

Mackenzie, George N. COLONIAL FAMILIES OF THE UNITED STATES OF AMERICA . . . FROM . . . 1607, TO . . . 1775 (Baltimore, Md.: Genealogical Publishing Co., 1966).

McAuslan, William, and Neff, Lewis, MAYFLOWER INDEX (The General Society of Mayflower Descendants, 1960). This has names of the original pilgrims, as well as some of their descendants.

Myers, Albert C. IMMIGRATION OF THE IRISH QUAKERS INTO PENNSYLVANIA, 1682-1750 (Baltimore, Md.: Genealogical Publishing Co., 1969 reprint).

PASSENGERS WHO ARRIVED IN THE UNITED STATES, SEPTEMBER 1821-DECEMBER, 1823 (Baltimore, Md.: Magna Carta Book Co., 1969).

Rupp, I. Daniel. A COLLECTION OF . . . THIRTY THOUSAND NAMES OF GERMAN, SWISS, DUTCH, FRENCH AND OTHER IMMIGRANTS IN PENNSYLVANIA FROM 1727 TO 1776 (Baltimore, Md.: Genealogical Publishing Co., 1965).

Savage, James. A GENEALOGICAL DICTIONARY OF THE FIRST SETTLERS OF NEW ENGLAND SHOWING THREE GENERATIONS OF THOSE WHO CAME BEFORE MAY 1692 (Boston, Mass.: Little, Brown & Co., 1860).

Sherwood, George. AMERICAN COLONISTS IN ENGLISH RECORDS. A GUIDE TO DIRECT REFERENCES IN AUTHENTIC RECORDS, PASSENGER LISTS NOT IN 'HOTTEN' . . . (London: G. Sherwood, 1932-33). This book concerns the period 1600-1800.

Ship Lists of Passengers Leaving France for Louisiana, 1718-1724, THE LOUISIANA HISTORICAL QUARTERLY, XIV (1931), pp. 516-520; XV (1932), pp. 68-77, 453-467; XXI (1938), pp. 965-978.

Skordas, Gust. THE EARLY SETTLERS OF MARYLAND (Baltimore, Md.: Genealogical Publishing Co., 1968).

Virkus, Frederick A., ed. IMMIGRANT ANCESTORS. A

LIST OF 2,500 IMMIGRANTS TO AMERICA BEFORE 1750 (Baltimore, Md.: Genealogical Publishing Co., 1963).

Whittemore, Henry. GENEALOGICAL GUIDE TO THE EARLY SETTLERS OF AMERICA WITH A BRIEF HISTORY OF THOSE OF THE FIRST GENERATION (Baltimore, Md.: Genealogical Publishing Co., 1967).

NOTE: Many more books and articles about immigrants have been published than I have listed here. I have given you these both to help you and so you would see the wide range of materials that have already been published on this subject.

23. INDEXES, GUIDES.

AMERICAN GENEALOGICAL-BIOGRAPHICAL INDEX TO AMERICAN GENEALOGICAL, BIOGRAPHICAL, AND LOCAL HISTORY MATERIALS (Middletown, Conn.: The Godfrey Memorial Library, 1949-1952; second series begun 1952, presently numbers 89 volumes, goes through the name Daisy Jacobs).

Colket, Meredith B., and Bridgers, Frank E. GUIDE TO GENEALOGICAL RECORDS IN THE NATIONAL ARCHIVES (Washington, D.C.: The National Archives, 1964).

Crowther, George R. SURNAME INDEX OF SIXTY-FIVE VOLUMES OF COLONIAL AND REVOLUTIONARY PEDIGREES (Washington, D.C.: National Genealogical Society, 1964).

DYER'S INDEX TO LAND GRANTS IN WEST VIRGINIA (Charleston, West Virginia: Moses W. Donally, 1896). This is an example of land grant indexes that can be found for most states.

Filby, P. William. AMERICAN AND BRITISH GENEALOGY AND HERALDRY (A SELECTED LIST OF BOOKS) (Chicago, Ill.: American Library Association, 1975).

HARVARD GUIDE TO AMERICAN HISTORY (Cambridge, Mass.: The Belknap Press of Harvard University Press, 1974) (2 volumes).

INDEX TO AMERICAN GENEALOGIES AND TO GENE-
ALOGICAL MATERIAL CONTAINED IN ALL WORKS
AS TOWN HISTORIES, COUNTY HISTORIES, LOCAL
HISTORIES, HISTORICAL SOCIETY PUBLICATIONS,
BIOGRAPHIES, HISTORICAL PERIODICALS, AND
KINDRED WORKS (Baltimore, Md.: Genealogical Publish-
ing Co., 1967 reprint).

NAME INDEXES. Look for these in the various libraries and
archives you visit. Many documents have been indexed in card
file form in depositories, but have not been issued in book form.

NEW ENGLAND HISTORICAL AND GENEALOGICAL
REGISTER; CONSOLIDATED INDEX, VOLS. 1-50 (Baltimore, Md.: Genealogical Publishing Co., 1972 reprint).

DICTIONARY CATALOG OF THE LOCAL HISTORY
AND GENEALOGY DIVISION, THE RESEARCH LI-
BRARIES OF THE NEW YORK PUBLIC LIBRARY (Bos-
ton, Mass.: G. K. Hall, 1974) (18 volumes).

24. INDIANS.

Curtis, Edward S. NORTH AMERICAN INDIANS: BEING
A SERIES OF VOLUMES PICTURING AND DESCRIB-
ING THE INDIANS OF THE UNITED STATES AND
ALASKA (N.Y.: Johnson Reprint Corporation, 1970) (20 vol-
umes).

25. JEWISH RESEARCH.

Howe, Irving. WORLD OF OUR FATHERS: THE JOUR-
NEY OF THE EAST EUROPEAN JEWS TO AMERICA
AND THE LIFE THEY FOUND AND MADE (N.Y.: Simon
and Schuster, 1976).

The Jewish Historical Archives, Jerusalem, Israel, and the Yivo
Institute of New York City both have a walth of material that
may be useful.

Joseph, Samuel. JEWISH IMMIGRATION TO THE
UNITED STATES FROM 1881 TO 1910 (New York: Arno
Press, 1969).

Rottenberg, Dan. FINDING OUR FATHERS; A GUIDE-BOOK TO JEWISH GENEALOGY (N.Y.: Random House, 1977). This includes tracing ancestry back to the old countries.

26. LIBRARIES.

AMERICAN LIBRARY DIRECTORY (N.Y.: R. R. Bowker Co., published annually since 1944).

Ash, Lee, and Lorenz, Denis, comps. SUBJECT COLLEC-TIONS (N.Y., 1967).

27. LOCAL HISTORY.

THE AMERICAN GENEALOGICAL-BIOGRAPHICAL INDEX TO AMERICAN GENEALOGICAL, BIOGRAPHI-CAL, AND LOCAL HISTORY MATERIALS (Middletown, Conn.: The Godfrey Memorial Library, 1952) (95 volumes published to date).

Filby, P. William. AMERICAN AND BRITISH GENE-ALOGY AND HERALDRY (A SELECTED LIST OF BOOKS) (Chicago, Ill.: American Library Association, 1975).

GENEALOGY AND LOCAL HISTORY: AN ARCHIVAL AND BIBLIOGRAPHIC GUIDE (Evanston, Ill.: The Associates, 1959).

Goodspeed's Book Shop, Inc., 18 Beacon St., Boston, Mass. 02108, has a catalog of Family and Local History, that includes over 2,000 local histories. Price at this writing, $1.50.

INDEX TO AMERICAN GENEALOGIES AND TO GENE-ALOGICAL MATERIAL CONTAINED IN ALL WORKS AS TOWN HISTORIES, COUNTY HISTORIES, LOCAL HISTORIES, HISTORICAL SOCIETY PUBLICATIONS, . . . [ETC.] (Baltimore, Md.: Genealogical Publishing Co., 1967 reprint).

Kane, Joseph. THE AMERICAN COUNTIES (N.Y.: The Scarecrow Press, Inc., 1960). This discusses county origins, dates of creation, organization, population, etc.

Peterson, Clarence S. CONSOLIDATED BIBLIOGRAPHY

OF COUNTY HISTORIES IN FIFTY STATES IN 1961 (Baltimore, Md.: Genealogical Publishing Co., 1963 reprint).

The Charles E. Tuttle Co., Inc., Rutland, Vermont 05701, sells a catalog called GENEALOGY AND LOCAL HISTORY. At this writing, it cost $2.00.

U.S. LOCAL HISTORIES IN THE LIBRARY OF CONGRESS: A BIBLIOGRAPHY (Baltimore, Md.: Magna Carta Book Co., n.d.) (4 volumes).

28. LOYALISTS.

NOTE: A loyalist was someone who actually fought on the British side during the Revolutionary War, most frequently in British uniform. Don't confuse a loyalist with someone who merely sympathized with the British cause.

Greenwood, Val D. THE RESEARCHER'S GUIDE TO AMERICAN GENEALOGY (Baltimore, Md.: Genealogical Publishing Co., 1974). On pages 440 through 443, Greenwood has an excellent list of books pertaining to loyalists.

Harrell, Isaac S. LOYALISM IN VIRGINIA (Durham, N.C.: Duke University Press, 1926).

Swem, Earl G., comp. VIRGINIA HISTORICAL INDEX (Roanoke, Virginia: Stone Printing Co., 1934-36) (2 volumes).

29. MAPS, ATLASES, ETC.

THE AMERICAN HERITAGE PICTORIAL ATLAS OF UNITED STATES HISTORY (N.Y.: American Heritage Publishing Co., Inc., 1966).

BULLINGER'S POSTAL AND SHIPPERS GUIDE FOR THE UNITED STATES AND CANADA: CONTAINING POST OFFICES AND RAILROAD STATIONS WITH THE RAILROAD OR STEAMER LINE ON WHICH EVERY PLACE, OR THE NEAREST COMMUNICATION POINT IS LOCATED, AND THE LIST OF RAILROADS AND WATER LINES WITH THEIR TERMINAL POINTS (Westwood, N.J.: Bullinger's Guides, Inc., published annually).

A LIST OF GEOGRAPHICAL ATLASES IN THE LIBRARY OF CONGRESS (Washington, D.C.: Library of Congress, 1909; reprinted 1968 by Paladin Press, New York).

Lunny, Robert M. EARLY MAPS OF NORTH AMERICA (1961). Deals with maps up to 1810.

Phillips, Philip L. A LIST OF MAPS OF AMERICA IN THE LIBRARY OF CONGRESS (1901).

Sealock, Richard B., and Seely, Pauline A. BIBLIOGRAPHY OF PLACE-NAME LITERATURE: UNITED STATES AND CANADA (Chicago, Ill.: American Library Association, 1967).

Special Libraries Association. MAP COLLECTIONS IN THE UNITED STATES AND CANADA (N.Y.: The Special Libraries Association, 1954).

Stephenson, Richard W., comp. LAND OWNERSHIP MAPS: A CHECKLIST OF NINETEENTH CENTURY COUNTY MAPS IN THE LIBRARY OF CONGRESS (Washington, D.C.: Library of Congress, 1967).

Wheat, Carl I. MAPPING THE TRANSMISSISSIPPI WEST, 1540-1861 (1957-1963) (5 volumes).

30. MILITARY RECORDS.

Brumbaugh, Gaius M. REVOLUTIONARY WAR RECORDS (Baltimore, Md.: Genealogical Publishing Co., 1967 reprint).

Colket, Meredith B., Jr., and Bridgers, Frank E. GUIDE TO GENEALOGICAL RECORDS IN THE NATIONAL ARCHIVES (Washington, D.C.: The National Archives, 1964).

Gwathmey, John H. HISTORICAL REGISTER OF VIRGINIANS IN THE REVOLUTION (SOLDIERS, SAILORS, MARINES) (Richmond, Virginia: Dietz Press, 1938). This is an example of the sort of book you should be able to find for nearly every state of the original 13.

Heitman, Francis B. HISTORICAL REGISTER OF OFFICERS OF THE CONTINENTAL ARMY (Washington,

D.C.: The Rare Book Shop Publishing Co., 1914).

Heitman, Francis B. HISTORICAL REGISTER OF THE U.S. ARMY, FROM . . . 1789, TO . . . 1889 (Washington, D.C.: The National Tribune, 1890).

Munden, Kenneth W., and Beers, Henry P. GUIDE TO FEDERAL ARCHIVES RELATING TO THE CIVIL WAR (Washington, D.C.: The National Archives, 1962).

Rider, Fremont, ed. AMERICAN GENEALOGICAL INDEX (Middletown, Conn.: The Godfrey Memorial Library, 1949-52; new series begun 1952, presently through volume 89, through name Daisy Jacobs). Indexes 1790 Census, 43 volumes of records of Revolutionary soldiers, and many family genealogies.

31. NEWSPAPERS.

AYER DIRECTORY OF NEWSPAPERS AND PERIODICALS (Philadelphia, Pa.: N.W. Ayer and Sons, published annually).

Brigham, Clarence S. HISTORY AND BIBLIOGRAPHY OF AMERICAN NEWSPAPERS, 1690-1820 (Hamden, Conn.: Shoe String Press, 1962).

Gregory, Winifred, ed. AMERICAN NEWSPAPERS 1821-1936—A UNION LIST OF FILES AVAILABLE IN THE UNITED STATES AND CANADA (N.Y.: H. W. Wilson Co., 1937).

Latham, Edward C. CHRONOLOGICAL TABLE OF AMERICAN NEWSPAPERS 1690-1820 (Worcester, Mass.: American Antiquarian Society, 1972).

Wynar, Lubomyr R. ENCYCLOPEDIC DIRECTORY OF ETHNIC NEWSPAPERS AND PERIODICALS IN THE UNITED STATES (Littleton, Colorado: Libraries Unlimited, 1972).

32. PENSIONS.

Metcalf, Frank J., and others, comps. INDEX OF REVOLUTIONARY WAR PENSION APPLICATIONS (Washington,

D.C.: National Genealogical Society, 1966).

33. PERIODICALS.

AYER DIRECTORY OF NEWSPAPERS AND PERIODI-CALS (Philadelphia, Pa.: N. W. Ayer and Sons, published annually).

Brown, Erma L. S. UNITED STATES GENEALOGICAL SOCIETIES AND PUBLICATIONS (Salem, Oregon: n.p., 1974).

Cappon, Lester J. AMERICAN GENEALOGICAL PERIOD-ICALS: A BIBLIOGRAPHY WITH A CHRONOLOGICAL FINDING-LIST (N.Y.: New York Public Library, 1964).

GENEALOGICAL PERIODICAL ANNUAL INDEX (Bladensburg and Bowie, Md.: Genealogical Recorders, published annually since 1962).

Jacobus, Donald L. INDEX TO GENEALOGICAL PERIOD-ICALS, VOL. I, 1858-1931; VOL. II, 1932-46; VOL. III, 1947-52 (Baltimore, Md.: Genealogical Publishing Co., 1973 reprint). This has a name index.

Meyer, Mary K., ed. DIRECTORY OF GENEALOGICAL SOCIETIES IN THE U.S.A. AND CANADA WITH AN AP-PENDED LIST OF INDEPENDENT GENEALOGICAL PERIODICALS (Published by M. K. Meyer, Rt. 10, Box 138-A, Pasadena, Md. 21122, 1976).

NEW YORK PUBLIC LIBRARY. This library subscribes to nearly 600 genealogical periodicals, and these can be seen at the library itself. For you who are west of the Mississippi, among other places, the Mormons in Salt Lake City subscribe to a large number of such periodicals as well.

PUBLISHER'S AND SEARCHER'S GUIDE (Published by House of York, 1323 Wylie Way, San Jose, Calif. 95130, annually since 1971). Contains, among many other things, references to genealogical periodicals.

STANDARD PERIODICAL DIRECTORY (Lexington, N.Y.: Oxbridge Publishing Co., published annually).

TOPICAL INDEX TO THE NATIONAL GENEALOGICAL SOCIETY QUARTERLY, VOLUMES 1-50, 1912-1962 (Washington, D.C.: The National Genealogical Society, 1964).

ULRICH'S INTERNATIONAL PERIODICALS DIRECTORY (N.Y.: R. R. Bowker Co., Published annually).

Here are some examples of Genealogical Periodicals, though these are only a few of the many:

THE AMERICAN GENEALOGIST (1232-39th St., Des Moines, Iowa 50311).

THE COLONIAL GENEALOGIST (The Hartwell Co., 945 2nd St., Hermosa Beach, Calif. 90254).

THE GENEALOGICAL HELPER (The Everton Publishers, Inc., P. O. Box 368, Logan, Utah 84321).

NEW ENGLAND HISTORICAL AND GENEALOGICAL REGISTER (101 Newbury St., Boston, Mass. 02116).

THE NEW YORK GENEALOGICAL AND BIOGRAPHICAL RECORD (122 E. 58th St., New York, N.Y. 10022).

34. QUAKERS.

Hinshaw, William W. ENCYCLOPEDIA OF AMERICAN QUAKER GENEALOGY (Ann Arbor, Mich.: Edwards Brothers, Inc., 1950) (6 volumes plus).

Myers, Albert C. IMMIGRATION OF THE IRISH QUAKERS INTO PENNSYLVANIA, 1682-1750 (Baltimore, Md.: Genealogical Publishing Co., 1969 reprint).

35. STATE RECORDS.

Rubincam, Milton, ed. GENEALOGICAL RESEARCH: METHODS AND SOURCES (Washington, D.C.: The American Society of Genealogists, 1960). This book has an excellent description of the records that are available in each state, and where they are located.

36. WPA PROJECT.

Child, Sargent B., and Holmes, Dorothy P. CHECK LIST OF

HISTORICAL RECORDS SURVEY PUBLICATIONS: BIB-LIOGRAPHY OF RESEARCH PROJECTS REPORTS, 1943 (Baltimore, Md.: Genealogical Publishing Co., 1969 reprint). This book outlines the findings of the Works Projects Administration's effort in the 1930's to record the locations of American records.

This work is also available on microfilm. See the catalog NATIONAL ARCHIVES MICROFILM PUBLICATIONS (Washington, D.C.: National Archives, 1974), under General Records of the Federal Works Agency, RG 162.

*   *   *   *   *

I realize that this book is packed with an enormous amount of information. Use it as you need it, a bit at a time, and have fun tracing *your* family tree!